Studies in Women and Religion/
Études sur les femmes et la religion : 2

Studies in Women and Religion /
Études sur les femmes et la religion

Studies in Women and Religion is a series designed to serve the needs of established scholars in this new area, whose scholarship may not conform to the parameters of more traditional series with respect to content, perspective and/or methodology. The series will also endeavour to promote scholarship on women and religion by assisting new scholars in developing publishable manuscripts. Studies published in this series will reflect the wide range of disciplines in which the subject of women and religion is currently being studied, as well as the diversity of theoretical and methodological approaches that characterize contemporary women's studies. Books in English are published by Wilfrid Laurier University Press.

Inquiries should be directed to the series coordinator, Pamela Dickey Young, Queen's Theological College, Queen's University, Kingston, ON   K7L 3N6.

STUDIES IN WOMEN AND RELIGION/
ÉTUDES SUR LES FEMMES ET LA RELIGION

Volume 2

The Work of Their Hands

Mennonite Women's Societies in Canada

Gloria Neufeld Redekop

Published for the Canadian Corporation for Studies in
Religion / Corporation Canadienne des Sciences Religieuses
by Wilfrid Laurier University Press

1996

This book has been published with the help of a grant from the Humanities and Social Sciences Federation of Canada, using funds provided by the Social Sciences and Humanities Research Council of Canada.

Canadian Cataloguing in Publication Data

Redekop, Gloria L. Neufeld, 1946-
    The work of their hands : Mennonite women's
societies in Canada

(Studies in women and religion = Études sur les femmes et la
religion ; v. 2)
Includes bibliographical references and index.
ISBN 0-88920-270-2

1. Mennonite women – Canada – Societies and clubs.
2. Women in church work – Canada – Mennonites.
I. Canadian Corporation for Studies in Religion.
II. Title.   III. Series: Studies in women and
religion (Waterloo, Ont.) ; v. 2.

BX8128.W64R44 1996   267'.449771   C96-930296-7

© 1996 Canadian Corporation for Studies in Religion /
        Corporation Canadienne des Sciences Religieuses

Cover design by Leslie Macredie

∞

Printed in Canada

The Work of Their Hands: Mennonite Women's Societies in Canada has been produced from a manuscript supplied in camera-ready form by the author.

Order from:
WILFRID LAURIER UNIVERSITY PRESS
Waterloo, Ontario, Canada   N2L 3C5

In memory of Anna Rose Bestvater Redekop (1901-1991)

"And let us not be weary in well doing: for in due season we shall reap, if we faint not. As we have therefore opportunity, let us do good unto all [people], especially unto them who are of the household of faith." (Gal. 6:9, 10)

"Was würde die Gemeinde tun, ohne diese treuen, fleiszigen Hände?" [What would become of the congregation without these faithful, hardworking hands?]

- Marie Dyck, *"Fleiszige Frauenhände,"*
Der Bote (30 November 1955): 46.

Table of Contents

List of Tables

List of Figures

Abbreviations

CMC Conference of Mennonites in Canada
MB   Mennonite Brethren
CWM Canadian Women in Mission
KM   *Kirchliche* Mennonite
MCC Mennonite Central Committee
WM   Women in Mission
WMA Women's Missionary Association
WA   Women's Association

Preface

Several years ago, when I first decided to examine the role of Mennonite women in the church, I realized that this could not be done without looking first at the role of Mennonite women's *Vereine* (the German word for "societies"). The story of these societies is virtually untold and Mennonite women who are members of *Vereine* have lamented the ways in which their work for the church through their societies has been devalued. It is the intention of this book to tell the story of Mennonite women's societies from the point of view of Mennonite women.

More people than I could mention have been an inspiration to me during the research and writing of this book. Many Mennonite women took the time and effort to not only answer survey questions, but also to search their own records for data that was not easy to retrieve. I received a number of handwritten copies of minutes of women's society meetings. In addition, their eagerness to have the history of their societies documented was a great encouragement to me during the more arduous phases of writing. My partner for life, Vern Neufeld Redekop, not only read preliminary drafts, but discussed the ideas with me at great length. Elisabeth Lacelle, Grace Jantzen and Linda Cardinal offered helpful suggestions along the way. Lucille Marr, Janet Hollingsworth, and Marlene Redekopp gave encouragement and support. My children, Quinn, Natasha, and Lisa, buoyed my spirits with their confidence that my project would be completed. Grandmother (Nanny) Anna Bestvater Redekop, who died before this book was published, was a long time active member of a Mennonite women's society in Herbert, Saskatchewan.

The research for this book was accomplished with the help of a grant from the Social Sciences and Humanities Research Council of Canada.

Mennonite Women's Society in Ukraine. Groups such as this one were the precursors of Mennonite Women's Societies in Canada. Photograph courtesy of Katharine Langeman and reproduced from the original by Eleanor Dyck.

Introduction

In the 1870s, when Russian Mennonites began to arrive in Canada, Mennonite women organized their own church societies, which they called *Vereine*[1]. While these were not without precedence in Europe, their growth in Canada was remarkable. They became the primary avenue of church involvement for Canadian Mennonite women, through which they have contributed vast amounts of energy, time, and financial resources to the mission activity of the church. Canadian Mennonite women, although restricted from leadership positions in the church, organized their own societies on the basis of a commitment inspired by the biblical text, because they, too, wanted to be obedient to God. These gendered societies functioned as a parallel church, becoming a context in which women could speak, pray, and creatively give expression to their own understanding of the biblical message.

This is the story of women's societies in two Russian Mennonite conferences in Canada: the Conference of Mennonites in Canada (CMC) and the Canadian Mennonite Brethren (MB). These Mennonite groups had their origins in the 1500s in the European Anabaptist movement, the radical left wing of the reformation.[2] Within this movement were religious communities which came to be called Amish, Hutterite, and Mennonite, the latter of which followed two distinct historical streams.[3] The first, known as Swiss Mennonites, originated in Switzerland, emigrated to Pennsylvania in the late 1600s and later to Ontario. A second stream, designated Russian Mennonites, originated in the Netherlands, went east to Prussia in the sixteenth century, to Russia in the late 1700s, and then to Canada in several waves of immigration, beginning in the late 1800s. There were 93,250 Canadian Anabaptist Mennonite members, both Swiss and Russian, in fifteen denominations in 1988, the year that the survey of Mennonite women's societies was conducted.[4] Those with historical roots in Russia comprised approximately seventy-seven thousand members in nine denominations (83 percent of Canadian Mennonites).[5] The largest two of these denominations are the CMC and MB. The CMC, numbering 29,192 members in 1988, an amalgamation of various Manitoba and Saskatchewan Mennonites, was established in 1903.[6] The MB, a church that originated as a renewal movement in Russia in 1860, had 25,395 members in Canada by 1988.

While similar women's societies were organized among Canadian Swiss Mennonites and other Russian Mennonite groups, I have chosen to limit myself to women's societies within the two largest Russian Mennonite groups in Canada. The first reason is that there are more Russian Mennonites in Canada than those of Swiss origin. Secondly, the CMC and MB together form 71 percent of all Russian Canadian Mennonites; therefore, an examination of women's societies within these two groups is representative of a high percentage of Russian Mennonites in Canada. A third reason for discussing only the experience of Russian Canadian Mennonite women is that the groups within the

1

Swiss Mennonite tradition may have exhibited significant differences in light of the fact that they came to Canada earlier. (A comparative study of women's societies among Swiss and Russian Mennonites could be a topic for future study.) Finally, a discussion of only Russian Mennonite women's societies allows for a manageable number of groups that are somewhat homogeneous.

Besides limiting this study to women's societies within the two largest Russian Mennonite groups, there is a limitation of time period. There were three major immigrations of Russian Mennonites to Canada: eight thousand people between 1874 and 1880, twenty thousand between 1923 and 1930, and seven thousand between 1947 and 1952.[7] I will examine all CMC and MB women's societies organized in churches formed between the first year of the first immigration period (1874) and the last year of the last immigration period (1952).

The decision to concentrate on women's societies in churches established during the immigration periods is related to their homogeneity. Since the concern of Mennonites during the immigration years was their own religious and cultural survival, they were occupied, first and foremost, with maintaining a strong Mennonite identity and keeping themselves separate from society. This is illustrated in the establishment of over twenty CMC and MB Bible schools and high schools in Canada between 1913 and 1947,[8] for the sake of "winning and keeping of the young people. Without them, all the leaders knew, there was no continuity for the Mennonite way of life, no perpetuity for the congregational communities and their values."[9] But after 1952, the focus gradually shifted from a concern for survival to a desire to establish new churches in Canada in areas where a critical mass of Mennonites did not exist. These churches were intended to reach out to people who were not Mennonite by ethnic origin, such as the French in Quebec.[10] Since the social and cultural reality in churches of other ethnic origins differed considerably from that of immigrant churches with Russian historical links, they are not included in this study.[11] It would require a separate study to measure the similarity of function of women's societies in these new churches to those of other immigrant churches.

Collecting archival materials entailed visiting three Canadian archives: The Centre for MB Studies (MB archives) in Winnipeg, Manitoba; Mennonite Heritage Centre (CMC archives) in Winnipeg, Manitoba; and the archives at Conrad Grebel College, a Mennonite college in Waterloo, Ontario. In these centres, I examined conference yearbooks, local church histories, and church periodicals. These included annual yearbooks of both the MB Church and the CMC for resolutions on women's role, annual reports of women's societies, and church histories written by local congregations. These brief histories, often written on in anniversary year of the church's establishment, sometimes contain a paragraph or two about women's societies in that church.

Church periodicals carry articles on Mennonite women's societies. I examined issues of the *Mennonite Brethren Herald*, *Mennonitische Rundschau*

(German Russian Mennonite periodical), the *Canadian Mennonite* (an independent inter-Mennonite periodical), and *Der Bote* (German Russian Mennonite periodical) for articles about Mennonite women's societies and women's role in general. In the case of the *Canadian Mennonite*, indexing was incomplete, so it was necessary to page through each issue to find relevant articles. Besides personal visits to archival libraries, I obtained on loan, all the issues of *The Mennonite Reporter* (an inter-Mennonite periodical which, for many members of the CMC, took the place of the *Canadian Mennonite* after 1971).

Besides archival work, other source material was gathered, some of which was received with survey responses. These included minutes and annual reports; financial reports; constitutions; personal letters; lists of members' names; themes of meetings; poems; and songs. Besides material that accompanied completed surveys, I collected the written histories of Canadian Women in Mission (CWM)[12] and provincial CMC women's societies; histories that record the activities of each local society within each province. I obtained access to the minutes of the South Saskatchewan MB Ladies Auxiliary, documented from its inception in 1959 to 1987. I visited the Central MB Church in Saskatoon, Saskatchewan, and gained access to reports of women's groups to the local congregation from 1976 to 1984; similar reports were obtained from the Herbert MB Church in Herbert, Saskatchewan, for the years 1973 to 1987. In Winnipeg, Manitoba, I examined archival material of the Women's Conference of the Manitoba MB Churches including correspondence and minutes of their organizational meeting in June 1976; minutes of their annual conferences in 1968, 1974, and 1976; and presidents' reports for the years 1968 and 1971 to 1974. I also obtained additional material from CWM offices in Winnipeg: CWM minutes of meetings for the years 1981 to 1987; CWM presidents' reports from 1978, and 1983 to 1987; and a list of CWM conference themes from 1953 to 1978. In Waterloo, Ontario, I consulted with a group of five female residents of the George Street Senior Home of the Waterloo/Kitchener United Mennonite Church on their experiences in the Mennonite church upon their arrival to Canada from Russia until the present. Antonio and Benjamin Redekopp of St. Catharines, Ontario, post-World War II immigrants from the Soviet Union, were interviewed about the purpose and work of Mennonite women's societies in Russia.

Despite the fact that I had gathered a remarkable amount of evidence, I realized that several aspects of the reality of women's societies were still missing. I had very little knowledge of how societies had changed through the years. I needed to hear from women themselves. For this reason, I decided to design a survey and distribute it to all CMC and MB women's societies in churches that had been established in the immigration years.

A survey instrument was developed in the fall of 1988[13] (see Appendix A). Questions were designed that would uncover aspects of *Vereine* not readily accessible in other source material. To ensure that survey questions would be unambiguous and that they would gather significant information for an understanding of women's societies, it was pre-tested by current members of Mennonite women's societies. Surveys were then sent to women's groups in eighty-five CMC and sixty-nine MB churches in Canada, comprising all CMC and MB societies currently in operation and organized in churches established during the immigration years. A cover letter which accompanied the survey form, indicated the intent of the research and requested additional information, including *Vereine* constitutions, annual reports, financial reports, and any other relevant documents. A second letter was sent two months later as a reminder to societies that had not yet responded.

Each women's group was requested to complete one survey. This meant that the number of surveys sent to each church varied, depending on how many women's groups were in each church. In the CMC, survey forms were sent to one of the *Verein* leaders in each church. It was possible to determine the number of women's groups in each CMC congregation since access to names of society leaders is readily available in the *Yearbook* of the CMC.[14] In MB churches, however, since a list of women's societies was not available, surveys were sent to the minister of each church, requesting him (they were all male) to give one survey form to each women's group in his church. Since there was no way of telling how many women's groups were in each church, an approximation was made on the basis of the number of members in each church. One survey per 250 MB church members was sent out, along with the request to photocopy and distribute the survey to other groups if there were more women's societies in the church than had been estimated. Phone calls were made in order to determine the total number of MB women's societies in each province.

The survey enabled information to be gathered that was not available in published or archival materials. It requested the name of the group and the year in which the group was organized. It asked how often the group met and whether the primary language of the group was German or English. Women were requested to indicate the purpose of their group, biblical texts and mottos underlying the group's motivation, components of meetings, projects undertaken, and methods of fundraising. The survey asked for the number of group members, the average attendance, the ages of women who attended, and the number of women employed outside the home. Groups were asked whether other church activities had affected attendance in their group. In addition, they were requested to name any women's groups in their congregations that had discontinued, and to state when and why they did so. Finally, respondents were asked to indicate specific changes that had occurred and to state when these had taken place. (See table 1 for rate by denomination and province.) Of the 304 Mennonite women's societies that could have completed surveys, responses were received from 188 groups. The return rate for CMC women's societies was 61 percent; for MB women's societies it was 63 percent.

Table 1
Percentage of Survey Responses

PROVINCE	CMC			MB		
	POSSIBLE RETURN	ACTUAL RETURN	PERCENT RETURN	POSSIBLE RETURN	ACTUAL RETURN	PERCENT RETURN
British Columbia	30	13	43	34	21	62
Alberta	17	12	71	10	7	70
Saskatchewan	53	34	64	25	20	80
Manitoba	54	44	78	31	19	61
Ontario	36	13	36	14	5	36
TOTAL	190	116	61	114	72	63

The survey tool served as a useful primary source in that a whole new body of knowledge about Mennonite women's societies was obtained. Hearing directly from 61 percent of all CMC and 63 percent of MB women's societies in Canada within congregations established in the immigration period, meant that a history could be written based on women's own voices and women's perception of their experiences within *Vereine*.

This is the story of Mennonite women's societies in Canada from the first years of Russian Mennonite immigration to Canada until the time of the survey in 1988, and into the 1990s. Part One sets the history of *Vereine* within the broader field of women's history and discusses the European background of Mennonite women's societies in Canada. It provides the historical context for the Canadian experience of *Vereine*. Part Two looks at the emergence of Mennonite women's societies in Canada and their establishment during the immigration years, centring on the reasons for organization within local churches and the primary foci of their groups. Part Three considers the meaning of membership in women's societies during a time period when virtually every woman in the Mennonite church was part of a church woman's society. It discusses the ways in which women's societies flowered between 1953 and 1969 and explores reasons for the growth. Part Four focuses on change and decline within Mennonite women's societies after 1970, an era when women's role within society was undergoing considerable change. It examines the elements of change within societies and probes the reasons for a decreasing interest in membership. The book ends with a look at trends in the 1990s.

Notes

1 *Vereine* is the German word for societies, clubs or associations. According to the South Western Ontario Women in Mission of the Conference of Mennonites in Canada, it signifies more than this: "It is a group that works together for a common goal . . . whose members give each other friendship and support." See Margaret Gossen Toews, ed., *South Western Ontario Women in Mission (1925-1987)* (Leamington: South Western Ontario Women in Mission, 1987), p. 5. Both in Europe and in the first decades of Mennonite immigration to Canada, many Mennonite women's groups were called *Vereine*. Since then most have changed to English names, although some groups which still use the German language have kept the designation of *Verein* (singular form). In this book, the words *Vereine* and societies will be used interchangeably.
2 Frank H. Epp, *Mennonites in Canada, 1786-1920: The History of a Separate People* (Toronto: Macmillan, 1974), p. 23.
3 Cornelius J. Dyck, ed., *An Introduction to Mennonite History* (Scottdale: Herald Press, 1967), pp. 26-162.
4 James E. Horsch, ed., *Mennonite Yearbook and Directory*, Vol. 79 (Scottdale: Mennonite Publishing House, 1990), p. 207.
5 Ibid.
6 Samuel F. Pannabecker, *Open Doors: A History of the General Conference Mennonite Church* (Newton: Faith and Life Press, 1975), pp. 146-149.
7 John A. Toews, *A History of the Mennonite Brethren Church* (Fresno: General Conference of Mennonite Brethren Churches, 1975), p. 153.
8 Pannabecker, *Open Doors*, p. 357, and Toews, *A History of the Mennonite Brethren Church*, pp. 173, 382.
9 Frank H. Epp, *Mennonites in Canada, 1920-1940: A People's Struggle for Survival* (Toronto: Macmillan, 1982), p. 447.
10 Toews, *A History of the Mennonite Brethren Church*, p. 174.
11 Prior to 1952, CMC and MB churches only existed in British Columbia, Alberta, Saskatchewan, Manitoba, and Ontario. Only CMC and MB women's societies in these provinces are included here.
12 Canadian Women in Mission is the name of the national organization of CMC women's societies.
13 Consent for conducting research involving human subjects was obtained from the University Human Research Ethics Committee, University of Ottawa, Ottawa, Ontario.
14 While the number of women's groups in each congregation varied from one to eighteen, most churches had one to three women's societies.

PART ONE

Background and Precedents

1

Women in Canadian Church History

Women have played a significant role in the history of the Christian church in Canada. This has included their work as women religious, participants in church women's societies, missionaries, and church leaders. Only recently has attention been paid to documenting what women have done in the church:

> It is commonly said that the Church would not have survived over the years without the support of women. While most people would agree with this observation, there has been little documentation of precisely what their contribution has been or what it has meant to the church as a whole or to any particular diocese.[1]

Previously, there has been a tendency to emphasize the contribution of significant individual women in the church, Roman Catholic women religious, and Protestant missionaries. It is only now that historians are beginning to look at the meaning of religion for ordinary women in Canadian churches.

The story of Canadian Mennonite women's societies, which is about ordinary Mennonite women, is situated first of all within the field of women in the Christian church in Canada. There has been more documentation of women religious in French-speaking Canada because of the prominence of religious communities. Historical work has focused on Roman Catholic women religious in Quebec and on the lives and work of individual women like Marguerite d'Youville and Élisabeth Bruyère.[2] While most work has been written from a denominational perspective, a few studies have offered an interpretation of women's role within the Roman Catholic community.[3] *Taking the Veil: An Alternative to Marriage, Motherhood, and Spinsterhood in Quebec, 1840-1920* studies the increase of women religious in Quebec from 1840 to 1920 in the context of the alternative it offered women in a society that valued women primarily as procreative beings.[4] *À la recherche d'un monde oublié. Les communautés religieuses de femmes au Québec de 1900 à 1970* is a feminist, sociological analysis of women religious in Quebec through periods of growth and decline of entrance into religious communities. It examines the identity of women who chose the vocation and characteristics of their families of origin.[5]

Ruth Compton Brouwer has noted that, until recently, "there has been a striking reluctance in English-speaking Canada to make women's experience in the realm of religion the *central* focus of scholarly study."[6] The focus has been on prominent religious women and preachers,[7] and home and foreign missionary activity.[8] Brouwer argues that because of the large numbers of women who participated in the foreign missionary movement, it is a subject worthy of documentation.[9]

Since the late 1980s, some attempts have been made to interpret women's religious experience in the light of the Canadian social historical context and from the perspective of gender and patriarchy in the church. In the recent monograph *A Sensitive Independence: Canadian Methodist Women Missionaries in Canada and the Orient, 1881-1925*, Rosemary Gagan makes the point that the experience of female Methodist missionaries was an alternative to marriage as well as an opportunity to develop professional skills.[10] Alison Kemper examines the vocation of deaconess in the Church of England as an expression of ideal womanhood.[11] In a discussion of early nineteenth century Methodist women preachers, Elizabeth Muir contends that ordination for women was allowed later in Canada than in the United States because of the religious and political climate in Canada.[12] Another recent interpretive study on women's ordination, by Valerie J. Korinek, suggests that the ordination of Lydia Gruchy in 1936 was not the end of a struggle, but the beginning of a continued struggle, an issue of patriarchy, religion, and gender in a church where males continued to dominate.[13]

An area of study that is only beginning to be addressed is the meaning of religion for ordinary women in Canada. Cecilia Morgan points to the lack of historiography on Canadian rural women and the meaning of religion in their lives. Her article shows how in the nineteenth century, Quaker women in Norwich had a relatively equal voice, in that they organized their own meetings, administered their own committees, and assumed responsibility for half of the Society's funds.[14] Pamela E. Klassen's recent book, concerning the meaning of religion for ordinary Canadian women,examines how two Mennonite women understood the importance of religion throughout their lives.[15] This book on Canadian Mennonite women's societies tells the story of the vast contribution to the church of ordinary Mennonite women, and at the same time, offers an interpretive framework for their *raison d'être*, suggesting that, because they were excluded from leadership roles in the larger church (and even denied voting privileges in the earlier years), Mennonite women's societies functioned for them, inadvertently perhaps, as parallel church.

The second field within which the story of Mennonite church women's societies is situated is that of the historiography of church women's societies in other Canadian Protestant churches. The work of these societies has been scantily documented even though these societies have contributed large amounts of money to the missionary program of the Protestant church. Brief accounts, written primarily by women who were members of these societies, record origins, goals, and activities of their organizations, beginning with the story of their establishment in the nineteenth and early twentieth centuries, and concentrating on a time span of anywhere from ten to 140 years.[16] These histories have several features in common. They are, for the most part, written from within women's societies themselves. These are the reports of the faithful, the members of women's societies. Anecdotal in style, the stories include a variety of details such as the names of women who were important to the success of societies, names of missionaries who were supported by women's groups, amount of money spent on mission projects, and lists of mission projects undertaken.

Although these stories of women's societies are primarily descriptive reports of group activities, they nonetheless supply evidence that these church women felt they were motivated by the call of God and thus, through their societies, could claim to be an integral part of the church body. The Woman's Auxiliary to the Board of Missions of the Church of England in Canada, organized in 1885, held strongly to "the claim of women to share in the work and responsibility of the church and missions."[17] The impetus for their work came from their sense of God's call, a call which was based on their own choice of biblical texts which gave direction to their groups. These included such texts as the following:

> For the earth shall be filled with the knowledge of the glory of the Lord,
> as the waters cover the sea. (Isa. 11:9)[18]
> The work of our hands, establish thou it. (Ps. 90:17)[19]
> She hath done what she could. (Mk. 14:8)[20]

Texts such as these gave women in Protestant women's societies a biblical ground for action.

Along with women in Presbyterian, Methodist, United, and Anglican churches, Mennonite women also wrote about the work of their societies. In the MB denomination, only a few histories of women's societies exist and these are merely short accounts buried within larger congregational histories,[21] while there is considerably more documentation of women's societies in the CMC. At the North American level, *Women in Search of Mission* documents the early beginnings of the General Conference Mennonite Church[22] women's missionary societies in the United States and their spread to Canada.[23] In Canada, in 1977, the twentieth anniversary of Canadian Women in Mission (CWM), the CMC national women's organization, was the occasion for the documentation of the work of CMC women's societies. Histories of provincial CMC women's groups in British Columbia, Alberta, Saskatchewan, Manitoba, and Ontario, as well as a history of CWM, were written at this time.[24] Typically, each provincial history lists all women's associations in the province and records such details as purpose of the group, year of organization, person responsible for establishment of the group, name given to the society, number of women attending, projects supported, methods of fundraising, and elements of regular worship. These are not unlike the anecdotal accounts of women's societies in other Protestant denominations. In common with other Protestant women's societies, women in Mennonite women's societies received their impetus for service from biblical teaching and were convinced that their work was an important contribution to the mission of the church.

While stories of women's societies are valuable for their accounts of the activities of church women's societies, only a few studies have analyzed Canadian Protestant women's church societies beyond a narrative description.

These have examined the value of women's societies to women who were part of them. They have also considered whether or not these societies functioned independently from the institutional church. How much freedom from male control did they have?

Pauline Bradbrook, in her article on the Church of England Women's Association in Newfoundland, shows how, throughout its existence, the women's association was controlled by the bishop and clergy. Nevertheless,

> they (the women) were creating a 'space' for themselves which was safe
> from all 'intruders' in a society that afforded no private space for
> women. . . . Members were able to learn skills within the association
> which they could not have gained elsewhere: handling money, running
> meetings, organizing social events, and making speeches.[25]

Shirley Davy, in her examination of the development of women's societies in the United Church of Canada from their early beginnings in the 1800s to the 1980s, agrees that women's societies gave women opportunities to develop their leadership skills and the power to organize.[26] Davy examines why women's societies were formed, why they thrived, and what their value was for women.

Wendy Mitchinson's article, "Canadian Women and Church Missionary Societies in the Nineteenth Century: A Step Towards Independence," documents the transition from financial accountability of women's associations to varying degrees of independence.[27] In her analysis of societies in the Presbyterian, Baptist, Methodist, and Church of England traditions, Mitchinson argues that while these women "did not consider themselves participants in the women's movement" and accepted "their role in terms of the traditional attributes of duty, service and self-denial,"[28] their associations provided a meaningful outlet for their energies and, in effect, contributed to women's increased role in society at large.[29] Brouwer agrees with Mitchinson that women's membership in church women's societies was enriching to them personally and spiritually, but in addition, became a context in which organizational skills could be developed.[30]

Marilyn Färdig Whiteley argues that although Methodist women in church women's societies found significant meaning in the work they did for the church, they were not necessarily able to do "about what they pleased."[31] In the late 1800s, women did not have access to their own money and, thus, had no choice but to raise funds through quilting and cooking. Whiteley suggests that women "could not freely determine either the goals for which they might labour or the methods they might use,"[32] and that this caused some frustration.

The examination of Mennonite women's societies in Canada has similarities to the work already done by Bradbrook, Davy, Mitchinson, and Whiteley. Mennonite women gained both personal and spiritual fulfillment through their participation within church women's societies. They not only learned to organize meetings and acquire leadership skills; I will suggest that their societies became a parallel church for them. While Mennonite women may not have expressed openly their frustration with the church institution, the story of their societies will allude to their hurt when their organizations were ridiculed and their work was not acknowledged as important.

The third context within which to place the story of Mennonite women's societies is the historiography of Mennonites in Canada. There has been only brief mention of women's societies in the written histories of Mennonites in Canada. Canadian Mennonite historiography has been primarily chronological and confessional. The most comprehensive and historically accurate studies of Mennonites in Canada are Frank H. Epp's two volumes, *Mennonites in Canada, 1786-1920: The History of a Separate People* and *Mennonites in Canada, 1920-1940: A People's Struggle for Survival.*[33] While these incorporate the history of all Canadian Mennonite traditions, including the CMC and MB, no mention is made of Mennonite women in the first volume. In the second, one reference to Mennonite women's sewing circles describes them as groups where women could help meet the physical needs of others and, at the same time, satisfy their own social needs.[34]

Separate histories of the MB and CMC have also been written. *A History of the Mennonite Brethren Church*, by John A. Toews, is a confessional account of the history of the Mennonite Brethren church from its beginnings in Europe to its continuation in the United States, Canada and other parts of the world.[35] Besides a brief reference to the deaconess movement, the number of women's groups in North America in 1968, and a small number of female missionaries, women are absent from the history.[36] While the story of home and foreign missions is told in some detail, the role of Mennonite women's associations who played a crucial role in supporting mission activity, is missing entirely.

One book has been written on the history of MB missions. In 1954, Mrs. H.T. Esau (designated by 'Mrs.' because 'H.T.' are her husband's initials) wrote *First Sixty Years of M.B. Missions.*[37] At the suggestion of a women's missionary society in an MB church in Kansas, Esau decided to write a book describing the work of MB missions around the world. Through storytelling, she gives a detailed chronicle of foreign mission work done by both married couples and single female missionaries. Her stories include the establishment of sewing circles, schools for girls, and homes for widows in foreign lands where MB missionaries worked. Recounting the work of these women's groups, she states: "they did things at home, such as raising chickens and vegetables and sewing clothing. Their mission sale in 1934 amounted to 76 rupees . . . It represented a great sum for those women."[38] While such details give significance to the role of women as missionaries, the author does not discuss the extent to which Mennonite women's societies in Canada were involved in the support of foreign missionaries.

The primary source for the history of the CMC is Samuel F. Pannabecker's *Open Doors: A History of the General Conference Mennonite Church.* Spanning the years 1860 to 1975, it combines Canadian and American

General Conference Mennonite history.[39] In the four pages devoted to women's associations, Pannabecker discusses their emergence in the United States in the late 1800s and consequent developments to 1975, praising missionary societies for their support of the mission program of the church.[40] Unlike other histories of Mennonites in Canada, he at least has recognized and acknowledged the value of women's contribution through women's societies, stating that "the Women's Missionary Association has been more than an association; it has been a multitude of consecrated and energetic women."[41]

A recent social historical work by Royden K. Loewen on the *Kleine Gemeinde*, a Russian Mennonite group who settled in Manitoba in 1874, is a good example of how the history of ordinary Mennonite women can be included within a larger history of the Mennonite people.[42] He discusses women's role as mothers, gardeners, and farm workers during the settlement years and acknowledges the importance of many 'ordinary' tasks that women usually performed as a matter of second nature. The establishment and work of women's church societies is briefly mentioned.[43]

While the history of Mennonite women has been virtually left out of Mennonite historiography, a few personal stories of Canadian Mennonite women have been published, all of them biographical in nature. The first was *The City Mission in Winnipeg*, in 1955, Anna Thiessen's personal story of the development of a home for immigrant girls who worked as domestics in Winnipeg in the early 1900s.[44] A few published letters and diaries document personal experiences of individual Mennonite women both in Russia and in the early years of immigration to Canada.[45] Three biographical compilations of Mennonite women's experience have also been published. In *Women Among the Brethren*, Katie Funk Wiebe attempts to depict the "courage, vision, sacrifice, and faith" of MB women as they immigrated from Russia to North America.[46] Based on data from personal files and interviews, only five of the fifteen stories are about Canadian MB women. *Full Circle: Stories of Mennonite Women*, by Mary Lou Cummings, is a collection of stories of Mennonite women from various Mennonite denominations;[47] only two out of nineteen women are Canadian. *Encircled: Stories of Mennonite Women*, by Ruth Unrau, a sequel to *Full Circle: Stories of Mennonite Women*, records stories of Mennonite women of the General Conference Mennonite Church.[48] Only two of the thirty-three stories are about Canadian women. Thus, even in the few biographical writings about the experience of Mennonite women, only a small percentage of them are about Canadian Mennonite women. Besides this, they do not mention the contribution of Mennonite women's societies to the church nor the value these held for Mennonite women.

Katie Funk Wiebe was one of the first to make explicit reference to the fact that women have been virtually absent from the documented history of Mennonites in Canada. She noted: "as I read Mennonite history books . . . women become a diffused segment of the mass of humanity which has no definitive characteristics . . . the names of women are missing almost entirely."[49] The history of Mennonite women, from their origins in the Netherlands in the 1500s to their immigration to Prussia, Russia, and Canada is scantily recorded due to several factors. First, until recently Mennonite historians have concentrated primarily on confessional history and history of church institutions. Wiebe has noted that historians do not try "to make sense of the lives of ordinary and powerless persons, particularly women, who were not part of the public record."[50] Referring to the connection between the historical record and women's primary role as wives and mothers, she stated that "the absence of historical material about Mennonite women may be symbolic of their role as wives, mothers, or maids, never entirely distinct from their servanthood position."[51]

A second reason for the lack of documented Mennonite women's history is the lack of available source material. This is especially true of eighteenth and early nineteenth century Russian Mennonite history, since documents were destroyed or made inaccessible due to the 1917 Bolshevik Revolution and subsequent civil war.[52] In addition, a number of women's societies did not keep records of meetings during their early years in Canada. For example, the Concordia Ladies Aid of Rosemary, Alberta, has no written records from 1930 to 1960.[53] Even those who did keep records did not necessarily give copies to archival libraries. If researchers wish to obtain minutes of Mennonite women's society meetings, they have to go to individual women's groups to retrieve them.

Third, in many instances, even when archival material is available, references to Mennonite women of the past are often designated by the names of men, with only a "Mrs." to indicate they were women.[54] This makes it difficult to identify these women and necessitates that the historian look for other source material. Mennonite historian Marlene Epp noted that there are problems finding and using archival materials when it concerns the history of Mennonite women's experience and contribution. She addresses the problem of sources in "Women in Canadian Mennonite History: Uncovering the 'Underside',", emphasizing the usefulness of non-traditional sources such as missionary society newsletters, interviews, conference yearbooks, and unpublished research papers.[55] It is from these sources that we learn the nature of women's involvement in the church; this is a time-consuming task.

Since women have been largely invisible in much of the writing about Mennonites, acknowledgement has not been given either to the extent of participation of Mennonite women within the context of *Vereine* nor to the significance of *Vereine* for women. Why did Mennonite women establish their own societies? What did the experience of participation in *Vereine* mean for Mennonite women? There is a gap in Mennonite history in that it does not include the history of Mennonite women; it is this gap that this book seeks to begin to fill.

The field of women's history, as we know it today, owes its existence partially to the growth of social history and partially to the women's movement.[56] The authors of *Canadian Women: A History* refer to this development:

> When feminists began to raise questions about the place of women in Canada, the absence of women from analysis became a challenge to historians. There was a growing awareness that the fact of gender made women's lives profoundly different from the lives of men. Women had an identity and a history, both barely represented in the standard studies. In the context of the women's movement and of a general widening of historical inquiry, Canadian women's history flowered.[57]

Since the rise of social history—a history focusing on ordinary people and one that claimed to be told "from the bottom up"—source material not previously considered valid, began to be accepted.[58] These included archival materials; routinely generated records; oral histories; registers; artifacts; autobiographies; local historical records; letters and diaries; the organizational records of women's clubs and religious organizations.[59] The acceptability of these sources for historiography meant that the documentation of the history of ordinary women began to be regarded as valuable and legitimate.

Prior to the influences of social history and the women's movement, historical writings about women did not ask questions about the uniqueness of women's experience nor did they examine the significance of gender roles.[60] Carroll Smith-Rosenberg refers to this earlier form of history as traditional women's history because it remained a descriptive history in areas which coincided with significant political events.[61] A few scholars further subdivide this style of traditional women's history. Natalie Zemon Davis discusses it under two categories.[62] The first, a style of history dating back to the fourteenth century, is "Women Worthies," histories written about queens and other notable women.[63] According to Davis, a second category of traditional women's history is that of biographies.[64] Gerda Lerner also divides the field of traditional women's history into two categories, but they are different from those of Davis.[65] What Davis refers to as "Women Worthies," Lerner calls "compensatory history," which she describes as histories of exceptional women of the past, written in order to compensate for the lack of the history of women within traditional historiography.[66] Joan Wallach Scott also refers to this as compensatory history, stating that

> in a sense, it could be said that the task of making women visible serves a compensatory purpose: it insists that women were actors in the past and provides information to prove that. Its effect is to supplement the picture we have traditionally had; sometimes even to change that picture.[67]

Lerner envisions a second category of traditional women's history, which she calls "contribution history," a history which details the contributions women have made at important male-defined historical junctures.[68] Elizabeth H. Pleck, on the other hand, refers to all of traditional women's history as "contribution history."[69]   Under this rubric she includes histories of exceptional women, biographies of individual women, and other histories which detail women's contribution to society, all written in order to compensate for their invisibility in historiography.[70]

Whatever we decide to call the earlier style of historical writing, Davis, Lerner, and Pleck agree that traditional women's history did give women a certain amount of visibility. Although anecdotal in nature, former histories of women at least have given "value to an experience that had been ignored (hence devalued)" and have insisted "on female agency in the making of history."[71] They have attempted "to fit women's past into the empty spaces of historical scholarship."[72] But these histories were lacking in several ways. First, they remained primarily histories of exceptional women. As Pleck observes, the experiences of ordinary women were still left out:

> The compensatory approach to women's history, no matter how necessary as a remedy for the invisibility of women and their accomplishments, places too much emphasis on those women whose lives departed most from the typical female experience through activism in public life.[73]

In the second place, traditional women's history was not told from a woman's perspective. It failed to portray women from their own point of view. In the earlier style of historiography, "never the subject of history, always the object, women lacked the power to include themselves in history and to define the terms for their inclusion."[74] A third difficulty with traditional women's history comes in the concept of periodization. Periods of time used in traditional historiography are not necessarily appropriate for women's history. Fourthly, former histories did not explore the issue of women's roles nor the consequences of gender.[75] Being strictly anecdotal, they failed to analyze gender or determine how history affected definitions of gender.[76] Women's history of the last two decades has begun to address what was missing in traditional women's history.

The field of women's history as we know it today is what Lerner refers to as "the true history of women," and Smith-Rosenberg calls the "New Women's History."[77] It is, first of all, a history which gives voice to all of women's experience. It is not only the story of exceptional women, but of ordinary women, presuming that "the ordinary as well as the unusual life experience of women as a group is worthy of historical inquiry."[78] Secondly, it is a history told from a female point of view. Pleck refers to this shift:

> Slowly, as the field has matured, historians of women's history have become dissatisfied with old questions and old methods, and have come up with new ways of approaching historical material. They have, for example, begun to ask about the actual experience of women in the past. This is obviously different from a description of the condition of women written from the perspective of male sources. . . . This shift from male-oriented to female-oriented consciousness is most important and leads to challenging new interpretations.[79]

Recently, there has been another shift in the field of women's history towards post-structuralist feminist thought which suggests that the category of 'women' is not easily constituted; it has multiple identities and is a complex cultural construction, intersecting with class, race, and ethnicity.[80]

In the third place, women's history utilizes those periodizations which are pertinent to women's life and experience:

> What feminist historiography has done is to unsettle . . . accepted
> evaluations of historical periods. It has disabused us of the notion that
> the history of women is the same as the history of men, and that
> significant turning points in history have the same impact for one sex
> as for the other.[81]

Fourthly, women's history deals with questions of women's position and gender roles, beginning with the assumption that there has been "difference, division, and inequality of male to female in history."[82] Acknowledging this reality, "we must from the outset apply what we know about women's position to our historical investigation. We cannot uncover the realities of women's past if we look at them as adjuncts to or minor participants in the male power."[83] Women's history explores the reasons for prescribed roles and addresses "the consequences of gender,"[84] one of which is that women often lived in two worlds, the male world and the female world. Elaine Leslau Silverman asks:

> Did Canadian women devise a culture of their own in which they could
> feel, not marginal or despised, but whole human beings? Did they live
> two kinds of lives, one in the male culture where they were controlled
> by tradition, fear, loyalty, and love, the other in a parallel society of
> women where their actions could range from intimacy to power?
> Historians will only understand women's lives when we recognize the
> dual nature of their existence. Women's historians have not yet begun
> to grasp that kind of tension.[85]

This question of a dual reality for women is of particular significance for the history of church women's societies. For church women there was a life within the institutional church, predominantly male controlled, and another life within the context of women's societies.

Implicit in the writing of women's history, as discussed above, is an approach which places women at the center of historical inquiry.[86] The first task is "the simple retrieval of women from obscurity."[87] So much of women's experience remains hidden. Brouwer suggests that the field of the history of women and religion needs to be broadened to include those whose history is currently not documented, including the study of native women's spirituality, the religion of working-class women, Catholic laywomen, Jewish women, and women who may have engaged in religious activities that we tend to discredit.[88] The history of Mennonite women's societies is also one that has been left out. It is about immigrant women, Protestant laywomen, and women who participated in activities associated with the domestic sphere, doing 'women's work'. While these women have not been discredited to the degree to which

Brouwer refers, there is evidence that Mennonite women's societies have been thought of in a disparaging way as contexts for women's 'gossip'. This study places these women in the center of historical inquiry.

A second task of a feminist viewpoint is to give women the opportunity to speak for themselves. When they give voice to their own reasons for their action, the results may be quite different than when they are treated as objects of historical inquiry. For example, Soha Abdel Kader, in her analysis of histories of Arab women, states that "questions designed to examine the role and position of women in Middle Eastern society from the standpoint of women themselves" need to be asked.[89] Kader shows that some studies, based on women's own words, have shown "how the conventional veil, rather than restricting women . . . is in fact a means they adeptly use to express themselves and their desires."[90] It may be the case that when Mennonite women are given a chance to tell their own story, the results may be different than anticipated.

Thirdly, a feminist approach offers "a description of women's oppression and a prescription for eliminating it."[91] A primary way in which women are oppressed is through silencing; the elimination of this kind of oppression is accomplished by giving them a voice. I concur with Ruth Pierson and Alison Prentice that

> one of the basic oppressions that women suffer is the silencing of their whole experience, both negative and positive. A basic injustice that feminists wish to redress, therefore, is inequality in terms of visibility. What feminists demand is the right to know and understand the experience of women and to have it analyzed, taken into account, recorded and valued.[92]

This history of *Vereine* gives Mennonite women a voice in an area of church involvement and spiritual growth that they have considered primary. In this sense it begins to end the oppression of the silence of their history.

Notes

1   Shirley Davy, Project Coordinator, *Women, Work and Worship in the United Church of Canada* (N.p.: The United Church of Canada, 1983), cited by Pauline Bradbrook, "A Brief Account of The Church of England Women's Association in Newfoundland," *Journal of the Canadian Church Historical Society* 28, 2 (October 1986): 93.

2   See *Les Ursulines de Québec, 1639-1989* (Québec: Le Comité de Fêtes du 350e anniversaire du fondation de l'École des Ursulines de Québec, 1989); Micheline D'Allaire, *Les Dots des religieuses au Canada français, 1639-1800. Étude économique et sociale* (Montréal: Hurtubise HMH, 1986); Francois Rousseau, *La Croix et le scalpel. Histoire des Augustines et de l'Hôtel-Dieu de Québec I: 1639-1892* (Québec: Septentrion, 1989); Sister Rita McGuire, *Marguerite d'Youville: A Pioneer for Our Times* (Ottawa: Novalis, 1982); Gilberte Paquette, *Dans le sillage d'Élisabeth Bruyère* (Vanier: Les Éditions L'Interligne, 1993); and Denise Robillard, *Émilie Tavernier-Gamelin* (Montréal: Éditions du Méridien, 1988).

3   See Marta Danylewyca, *Taking the Veil: An Alternative to Marriage, Motherhood, and Spinsterhood in Quebec, 1840-1920* (Toronto: McClelland and Stewart, 1987); Nicole Laurin, Danielle Juteau, and Lorraine Duchesne, *À la recherche d'un monde oublié. Les communautés religieuses de femmes au Québec de 1900 à 1970* (Montréal: Le Jour, 1991); Anita Caron, ed., *Femmes et pouvoir dans l'Église* (Montréal: VLB Éditeur, 1991); and Elisabeth J. Lacelle, éd., *La femme et la religion au Canada français* (Montréal: Bellarmin, 1979).
4   Danylewyca, *Taking the Veil.*
5   Laurin, Juteau, and Duchesne, *A la recherche d'un monde oublié.*
6   Ruth Compton Brouwer, "Transcending the 'unacknowledged quarantine': Putting Religion into English-Canadian Women's History," *Journal of Canadian Studies* 27, 3 (Fall, 1992): 47.
7   Lois Wilson, *Turning the World Upside Down: A Memoir* (Toronto: Doubleday Canada, 1989); Ruth Compton Brouwer, "The 'Between-Age' Christianity of Agnes Machar," *Canadian Historical Review* 65, 3 (1984): 347-370; Mary E. Hallett, "Nellie McClung and the Fight for the Ordination of Women in the United Church of Canada," *Atlantis* 4, 2 (Spring 1979): 2-16; Carol L. Hancock, "Nellie L. McClung: A Part of a Pattern," in *Prairie Spirit: Perspectives on the Heritage of the United Church of Canada in the West,* ed. Dennis L. Butcher et al. (Winnipeg: University of Manitoba Press, 1985); Elizabeth Muir, *Petticoats in the Pulpit: Early Nineteenth-Century Methodist Women Preachers in Upper Canada* (Toronto: United Church Publishing House, 1991); and Marilyn Whiteley, "Modest, Unaffected and Fully Consecrated: Lady Evangelists in Canadian Methodism, 1884-1900," Canadian Methodist Historical Society, *Papers* 6 (1987).
8   See Rosemary Gagan, *A Sensitive Independence: Canadian Methodist Women Missionaries in Canada and the Orient, 1881-1925* (Kingston and Montreal: McGill-Queen's University Press, 1992); Elizabeth Muir, "The Bark Schoolhouse: Methodist Episcopal Missionary Women in Upper Canada, 1827-1833," and Geoffrey Johnson, "The Road to Winsome Womanhood: The Canadian Presbyterian Mission among East Indian Women and Girls in Trinidad, 1868-1939," in John S. Moir and C.T. McIntire, eds., *Canadian Protestant and Catholic Missions, 1820s-1960s: Historical Essays in Honour of John Webster Grant* (New York: Peter Lang, 1988); and Ruth Compton Brouwer, *New Women for God: Canadian Presbyterian Women and India Missions, 1876-1914* (Toronto: University of Toronto Press, 1990).
9   Brouwer, *New Women for God.*
10 Gagan, *A Sensitive Independence.*
11 Alison Kemper, "Deaconess as Urban Missionary and Ideal Woman: Church of England Initiatives in Toronto, 1890-1895," in Moir and McIntire, eds., *Canadian Protestant and Catholic Missions.*
12 Muir, *Petticoats in the Pulpit.*
13 Valerie J. Korinek, "No Women Need Apply: The Ordination of Women in the United Church, 1918-65," *Canadian Historical Review* 74, 4 (1993): 473-509.
14 Cecilia Morgan, "Gender, Religion, and Rural Society: Quaker Women in Norwich, Ontario, 1820-1880," *Ontario History* 82, 4 (December 1990): 273-287.
15 Pamela E. Klassen, *Going by the Moon and the Stars: Stories of Two Russian Mennonite Women* (Waterloo: Wilfrid Laurier University Press, 1994).
16 See Harriet Louise Platt, *The Story of the Years: A History of the Woman's Missionary Society of the Methodist Church, Canada, 1881-1906,* 2 vols. (Toronto: Women's Missionary Society, 1908); Mrs. W.H. Graham, *Forty-Five Years Effort of the Woman's Missionary Society of the Methodist Church of Canada, 1881-1925* (Toronto: Women's Missionary Society, n.d.); Jean G. Campbell, *A Lively Story: Historical Sketches of the Women's Missionary Society (Western Division) of the Presbyterian Church in Canada*

1864-1989 (N.p., 1989); Mary Cramp, *Retrospect, A History of the Formation and Progress of the Women's Missionary Aid Societies of the Maritime Provinces* (N.p., 1892); Jean Gordon Forbes, *Wide Windows: The Story of the Woman's Missionary Society of the United Church of Canada* (N.p.: Women's Missionary Society, 1951); Mary Kinley Ingraham, *Seventy-Five Years Historical Sketch of the United Baptist Woman's Missionary Union in the Maritime Provinces of Canada* (Kentville: Kentville Publishing, n.d.); Mary McKerihen, *A Brief History Relative to the Growth and Development of Woman's Associations from Local to Presbytery to Conference to Dominion Courts. 1913-1943* (Toronto: Woman's Association Council of the United Church of Canada, 1943); Mrs. Garfield Arthur Platt, *The Story of the Woman's Auxiliary in the Diocese of Ontario: 1885-1961* (N.p., 1961); and Earl Merrick, *These Impossible Women. The Story of the United Baptist Women's Missionary Union of the Atlantic Provinces* (Fredericton: N.p., 1970).

17 Platt, *The Story of the Woman's Auxiliary in the Diocese of Ontario*, p. 12.

18 Ingraham, *Seventy-Five Years Historical Sketch*, p. 38.

19 McKerihen, *A Brief History*, p. 47.

20 Platt, *The Story of the Woman's Auxiliary in the Diocese of Ontario*, p. 2.

21 One example is *Leamington Mennonite Brethren Church* (N.p., n.d.).

22 The General Conference Mennonite Church is the North American organization to which both the American General Conference Mennonites and the CMC belong.

23 Gladys V. Goering, *Women in Search of Mission: A History of the General Conference Mennonite Women's Organization* (Newton: Faith and Life Press, 1980).

24 Katie Hooge, *The History of the Canadian Women in Mission (1952-1977)* (Winnipeg: Canadian Women in Mission, 1977); Hildegard Fiss, *The Story of Women in Mission (Southwest Ontario)* (N.p., 1976); Anita Froese, *Manitoba Mennonite Women in Mission (1942-1977)* (Winnipeg: Manitoba Mennonite Women in Mission, 1977); Mary Bartel, *Saskatchewan Women in Mission* (N.p.: Saskatchewan Women in Mission, 1977); Anne Neufeld, ed., *History of Alberta Mennonite Women in Mission (1947-1977)* (Coaldale: Alberta Mennonite Women in Mission, 1977); and Martha Rempel, *History of B.C. Mennonite Women in Mission (1939-1976)* (Chilliwack: British Columbia Mennonite Women in Mission, 1976). Ontario Women in Mission later updated their histories, resulting in *Ontario Women in Mission (1946-1986)* (N.p.: Ontario Women in Mission, 1986); and Toews, ed., *South Western Ontario Women in Mission*.

25 Bradbrook, "A Brief Account of The Church of England Women's Association in Newfoundland," p. 101.

26 Davy, *Women, Work and Worship in the United Church of Canada*, pp. 73-74.

27 Wendy Mitchinson, "Canadian Women and the Church Missionary Societies in the Nineteenth Century: A Step Towards Independence," *Atlantis* 2 (Spring 1977): 73.

28 Ibid.

29 Ibid.

30 Brouwer, *New Women for God*, p. 189.

31 Marilyn Färdig Whiteley, " 'Doing Just About What They Please': Ladies' Aids in Ontario Methodism," *Ontario History* 82, 4 (December 1990): 300.

32 Ibid.

33 Epp, *Mennonites in Canada, 1786-1920* and *Mennonites in Canada, 1920-1940*.

34 Epp, *Mennonites in Canada, 1920-1940*, p. 458.

35 Toews, *A History of the Mennonite Brethren Church*, p. xi.

36 Ibid., pp. 94, 213, 226, 313, 400-436.

37 Mrs. H.T. Esau, *First Sixty Years of M.B. Missions* (Hillsboro: Mennonite Brethren Publishing House, 1954).

38 Ibid., pp. 49, 67, 205, 354.

39 Pannabecker, *Open Doors*.

40 Ibid., pp. 288-291.

41 Ibid., p. 291.

42 Royden K. Loewen, *Family, Church, and Market: A Mennonite Community in the Old and New Worlds, 1850-1930* (Toronto: University of Toronto Press, 1993).

43 Ibid., pp. 173, 233.

44 Anna Thiessen, *The City Mission in Winnipeg*, trans. Ida Toews (Winnipeg: Centre for MB Studies, 1991).

45 Anna Baerg, *Diary of Anna Baerg (1916-1924)*, trans. and ed. Gerald Peters (Winnipeg: Canadian Mennonite Brethren Bible College, 1985); Anna Reimer Dyck, *Anna: From the Caucasus to Canada*, trans. and ed. Peter J. Klassen (Hillsboro: Mennonite Brethren Publishing House, 1979); and Susan Toews, *Letters From Susan: A Woman's View of the Russian Mennonite Experience (1928-1941)*, trans. and ed. John B. Toews (North Newton: Bethel College, 1988).

46 Katie Funk Wiebe, ed., *Women Among the Brethren* (Hillsboro: Mennonite Brethren Publishing House, 1979), p. viii.

47 Mary Lou Cummings, ed., *Full Circle: Stories of Mennonite Women* (Newton: Faith and Life Press, 1978).

48 Ruth Unrau, *Encircled: Stories of Mennonite Women* (Newton: Faith and Life Press, 1986).

49 Lawrence Klippenstein and Julius G. Toews, eds., *Mennonite Memories: Settling in Western Canada* (Winnipeg: Centennial Publications, 1977), pp. 312-314.

50 Katie Funk Wiebe, "Mennonite Brethren Women: Images and Realities of the Early Years," *Mennonite Life* 36, 3 (September 1981): 22.

51 As quoted in Lawrence Klippenstein and Julius G. Toews, eds., *Manitoba Mennonite Memories* (Altona: Manitoba Mennonite Centennial Committee, 1974), p. 250.

52 John B. Toews, *Czars, Soviets and Mennonites* (Newton: Faith and Life Press, 1982), p. 213.

53 "Concordia Ladies Aid for 1988," Rosemary Mennonite Church, Rosemary, Alberta, 1988.

54 See the reference to "Mrs. H.T. Esau" on page 23 of this manuscript.

55 Marlene Epp, "Women in Canadian Mennonite History: Uncovering the 'Underside,' " *Journal of Mennonite Studies* 5 (1987): 90-107.

56 Carroll Smith-Rosenberg, "The New Woman and the New History," *Feminist Studies* 3 (1975): 188.

57 Alison Prentice et al., *Canadian Women: A History* (Toronto: Harcourt Brace Jovanovich Canada, 1988), p. 12.

58 Peter N. Stearns, "The New Social History: An Overview," in *Ordinary People and Everyday Life: Perspectives on the New Social History*, ed. James B. Gardner and George Rollie Adams (Nashville: American Association for State and Local History, 1983), p. 4.

59 Gerda Lerner, "New Approaches to the Study of Women in American History," in *Liberating Women's History: Theoretical and Critical Essays*, ed. Berenice A. Carroll (Chicago: University of Illinois Press, 1976), p. 353; Georg G. Iggers and Harold T. Parker, eds., *International Handbook of Historical Studies: Contemporary Research and Theory* (Westport: Greenwood Press, 1975), p. 182; and Stearns, "The New Social History, p. 11.

60 Smith-Rosenberg, "The New Woman and the New History," p. 186.

61 Ibid., p. 186.

62 Natalie Zemon Davis, " 'Women's History' in Transition: The European Case," *Feminist Studies* 3 (Spring-Summer 1976): 83.

63 Ibid.

64 Ibid., pp. 83-84.

65 Gerda Lerner, "Placing Women in History: A 1975 Perspective," in *Liberating Women's History*, pp. 357-58.

66 Ibid.

67 Joan Wallach Scott, "The Problem of Invisibility," in *Retrieving Women's History: Changing Perceptions of the Role of Women in Politics and Society*, ed. Jay S. Kleinberg (Great Britain: Berg Publishers, 1988), p. 12.

68 Lerner, "Placing Women in History," p. 358.

69 Elizabeth H. Pleck, "Women's History: Gender as a Category of Historical Analysis," in *Ordinary People and Everyday Life*, pp. 52-54.

70 Ibid.

71 Joan Wallach Scott, *Gender and the Politics of History* (New York: Columbia University Press, 1988), p. 18.

72 Lerner, "Placing Women in History," pp. 358-360.

73 Pleck, "Women's History," p. 54.

74 Lerner, "Placing Women in History," p. 52.

75 Davis, " 'Women's History' in Transition," p. 90.

76 Ibid., p. 84.

77 Lerner, "Placing Women in History," p. 359, and Smith-Rosenberg, "The New Woman and the New History," p. 188.

78 Pleck, "Women's History," p. 55.

79 Ibid., p. 362.

80 For a discussion of post-structuralism and feminism, see Judith Butler, *Gender Trouble: Feminism and the Subversion of Identity* (New York: Routledge, 1990), and Denise Riley, *"Am I that Name?" Feminism and the Category of 'Women' in History* (Minneapolis: University of Minnesota, 1988). Since this social history of Mennonite women's societies is not a discussion of the oppression of Mennonite women, neither does it claim that the experience of Mennonite women is universal, but rather is situated within a particular religious group and culture, the post-structuralist debate does not materially affect it.

81 Joan Kelly, *Women, History & Theory: The Essays of Joan Kelly* (Chicago: University of Chicago Press, 1984), p. 3.

82 Pleck, "Women's History," p. 57.

83 Hilda Smith, "Feminism and the Methodology of Women's History," in *Liberating Women's History*, p. 383.

84 Davis, " 'Women's History' in Transition," p. 90.

85 Elaine Leslau Silverman, "Writing Canadian Women's History, 1970-82: An Historiographical Analysis," *Canadian Historical Review* 63, 4 (1982): 521.

86 Ruth Pierson and Alison Prentice, "Feminism and the Writing and Teaching of History," *Atlantis* 7,2 (Spring, Printemps 1982): 41.

87 Ibid.

88 Brouwer, "Transcending the 'unacknowledged quarantine,' " p. 57.

89 Soha Abdel Kader, "The Role of Women in the History of the Arab States," in *Retrieving Women's History*, p. 85.

90 Ibid., p. 86.

91 Alison M. Jaggar and Paula Rothenberg Struhl, *Feminist Frameworks: Alternative Theoretical Accounts of the Relations between Women and Men* (New York: McGraw-Hill, 1978), p. xi.

92 Pierson and Prentice, "Feminism and the Writing and Teaching of History," p. 38.

2

European Context

In order to understand the establishment and development of women's societies among Russian Mennonite immigrants in Canada, it is important to examine the historical background for precedents that may have helped to shape their initial formation. This takes us back to the genesis of the Anabaptist movement in the Netherlands in the 1550s, since it is from Dutch Anabaptism that the religious tradition of Russian Mennonites originates.

While our knowledge of the role of women in Dutch Anabaptism is very limited, three major sources are helpful. *The Complete Writings of Menno Simons* contains all the written works of Menno Simons, a Dutch Anabaptist leader.[1] From this source we can determine what he believed and taught about women's role. A second source, *Martyrs' Mirror of the Defenseless Christians*, deals with Christian martyrdom from the first to the sixteenth centuries.[2] Included are stories of martyrs, official court records, and personal letters of Dutch Anabaptist martyrs. It is from this source that we learn what women believed and to what extent they participated in the Anabaptist movement of the 1500s. A third useful source is the Mennonite Encyclopedia which contains entries on the role of Anabaptist women in the Netherlands.[3]

The role that was prescribed for Dutch Anabaptist women was not necessarily consistent with their behavior. In his treatise of 1556, "The True Christian Faith," Simons used ten examples of biblical characters to illustrate the qualities of true faith.[4] In one of these, he gave this advice to Christian women:

> Do not adorn yourselves with gold, silver, costly pearls and embroidered hair, and expensive, unusual dress. . . . Be obedient to your husbands in all reasonable things. . . . Remain within your houses and gates unless you have something of importance to regulate, such as to make purchases, to provide in temporal needs, to hear the Word of the Lord, or to receive the holy sacraments, etc. Attend faithfully to your charge, to your children, house, and family.[5]

Clearly, women's place was to be in the domestic sphere. In one of his letters addressed to a widow, Simons referred to "the weakness of the womanly nature" and encouraged the widow to "carry on bravely . . . take good care of your labor, your household and children. Diligently avoid all immodesty, gossip, pride, and vanity."[6] In another letter, addressed to the wife of a man who was contemplating becoming a pastor of a church, Simons voiced disapproval of her opposition to her husband's calling as pastor, stating that "the love to God and our brethren must be considered first of all."[7] From these few references to women in Menno Simons' writings, we can gather that he believed women's primary role was in the home, that women should be supportive of their husbands' calling to pastoral work, and that they should dress in a simple, modest fashion. While this gives us an indication of what was expected of women, other sources tell us whether the prescription of women was consistent with their behavior.

The entries in *Martyrs' Mirror of the Defenseless Christians* and the *Mennonite Encyclopedia* indicate that Anabaptist women in the Netherlands were well-versed in the Bible.[8] They read theological documents and wrote testaments of faith to their children.[9] In one instance, a particular woman appeared to be more skilled in locating biblical texts than her minister husband, for "whenever he could not find a passage, he would ask his wife, Claudine, who would at once clearly indicate to him what he sought."[10] Because of the emphasis on the authority of scripture and the priesthood of all believers at the time of the Reformation, it became important for men, women, and children to learn to read and write. Even an opponent of Anabaptism took note of their sudden ability to read.[11] Along with reading the biblical text, women boldly spoke of their faith.[12] When brought to trial, both women and men defended their positions with lengthy quotations from the Bible.[13] In a mixed group of men and women, speaking was not necessarily left to the men. In fact, on one occasion, when four women together with two men were brought to trial, "the two brethren, Bruyn and Anthonis the weaver, who were brought out with them, were very sorrowful and did not speak; the women, however, spoke much and greatly reproved the monks."[14] Besides speaking of their faith, women composed religious music. One such song writer was Soetken Gerrits of Rotterdam who composed approximately one hundred hymns which, in 1592, were compiled into a hymn book entitled *Nieu Gheestelijck Liedboexken*.[15]

Even though women seemed free to speak of their faith in public and they were addressed as "coworkers and followers of the gospel,"[16] men were the elders in the church and heads of households. They were responsible for the spiritual-well being of church members; men, women and children were expected to submit to male elders. In the home, the husband was head of wife and children, just as Christ was the head of the church.[17] It was the husband's responsibility to nurture the family through scripture and prayer. Husbands were to love, protect, and support their wives; wives were to be submissive and obedient to husbands. However, in spite of the fact that men were the official church leaders, some women did hold church leadership positions.[18] One such woman was Elizabeth of Leeuwarden, a leading figure in Dutch Anabaptism, who travelled and worked with Menno Simons.[19] In her court trial she is referred to as *Leeraresse*, (teacheress), someone who taught publicly. Aeffgen Lystyncx and Elizabeth Dirks also taught and preached in Anabaptist meetings.[20] Lystyncx was said to have organized Anabaptist conventicles and is called a "prophetess."[21] Another woman, Digna Pieters, "held conventicles, contrary to the faith, holy sacraments, and other services and ceremonies of the holy (Roman) church."[22] These examples indicate that at least some women were involved in leadership roles in early Dutch Anabaptism.

While Anabaptist women experienced a certain amount of liberation at the beginning of the movement, there was a return to subservient roles as soon as the church became institutionalized. Feminist author, Marilyn French, refers to this phenomenon when she states that "in conditions of severe hardship, like famine and war, women and men struggle together for survival; in periods of tight control, men exclude women."[23] The sense of freedom women had in the early years of Anabaptism was soon lost when Mennonites no longer had to fear for their lives.

One of the separate roles for women that developed in the late 1500s, after persecution in the Netherlands had abated, the diaconate.[24] The following description of the role of deaconess in Dutch Anabaptism is cited in the Dordrecht Confession of Faith of 1632, the basis of union of Frisian and Flemish Mennonites in the Netherlands:

> Also that honorable old widows be ordained and chosen as servants, who besides the almoners, are to visit, comfort, and take care of the poor, the weak, the afflicted, and the needy, as also to visit, comfort, and take care of widows and orphans; and further to assist in taking care of any matters in the church that properly come within their sphere, according to their best ability.[25]

Duties of the deaconess seemed to include care of the sick and needy. It is not clear what else was considered part of her work, but it appears that duties were an extension of women's role in the home; they were caregivers. The concern of the church was that they remain "properly . . . within their sphere."[26]

In the early years of Dutch Anabaptism, we find no evidence that women formed their own societies. The work that women did later on in the context of women's societies, such as giving resources to the less privileged, was at this time considered an integral part of true discipleship for both men and women.[27] At secret meetings in cellars and forests, money, food, and clothing for the needy were placed in boxes and sacks. These were then distributed by the leading minister or an appointed *Seckelmeister* (treasurer).[28] This connection between discipleship and care for the needy were two categories of experience that later figured prominently in the establishment and development of Mennonite women's societies. However, it is not until three hundred years later, after immigration to Russia, that references are made to the organization of these societies.

As Mennonites[29] fled persecution in the Netherlands, some as early as 1540, and immigrated to Prussia and later to Russia, the church moved towards institutionalization, and restrictions in women's church roles became more pronounced.[30] For the two hundred years of Mennonite residence in Prussia it is difficult to determine the nature of women's participation in church life because of the lack of source material, but we do have some indication that male authority became firmly entrenched. One indication of this is in the practice of

Bruderschaft (a decision-making body composed of all adult males in the church).[31] Male dominance was symbolized in the design of the church interior. Males sat on one side of the church on elevated seats; females sat on the other side of the church at a lower level.[32] Women were not allowed to vote in the church nor did they officially have any influence in church decisions. The *Bruderschaft* decided " all important financial matters, the excommunication of erring and readmission of penitent members, matters of dogma and church governance, and the acceptance or rejection of the church council's resolutions. . . . The brotherhood elects its elders, teachers and deacons."[33] There is no evidence that Mennonite women's societies existed at this time.

Mennonites remained in Prussia until the late 1700s. Here they were granted military exemption, were relatively free to practise their religion, and could purchase as much land as they wished. They continued until 1744, when Frederick the Great passed a law forbidding further purchase of land by the Mennonites. Therefore, it is understandable that Mennonite people were eager to go when Catherine the Great of Russia invited Prussian communities to come to Russia in 1789. Within fifty years, half the Mennonite Prussian population, approximately six thousand people, had immigrated to Russia.[34]

Poor and landless Mennonites were the first to leave Prussia for Russia where they were granted their own educational system, the right to local self-government, religious freedom, and exemption from military service. By 1789, eight Mennonite villages had been established in the Chortitza colony and by 1812, Molotschna colony had twenty villages.[35] Unique in its emphasis on spiritual renewal was the village of Gnadenfeld, one of the two major administrative and communication centres of Mennonites in the Molotschna colony. In Gnadenfeld, "the consecration of children, mission festivals, emphasis on temperance, and other practices generally unknown among Mennonites were adhered to in Gnadenfeld."[36] They met for worship so often that their opponents called them "meeting-goers"; besides weekly meetings they held monthly conferences.[37] An influential figure was the Lutheran-Pietist pastor, Eduard Wüst, who in 1945 came to minister in the German-Lutheran congregation of Neuhoffnung, south of Molotschna. He was frequently invited to speak at Mennonite mission festivals in Gnadenfeld and elsewhere.[38] It was at this time that Mennonites became interested in supporting a foreign missions program and it was in this context that Mennonite women's societies had their birth. At one of the Gnadenfeld events

> it was agreed to organize a Women's Society during the winter months to enable the women to meet once a week in the afternoons to knit and sew for missions. . . . The working period of the sisters was preceded by prayer and singing led by a brother; missionary news was read from time to time while the women worked. The meetings closed with song and prayer.[39]

While we cannot be sure of the exact date that Mennonite women's societies were established here, we know that it occurred between 1835, the settlement of Gnadenfeld, and the late 1840s, when the influence of Eduard Wüst was felt in the village. With their roots in the spiritual renewal movement in Gnadenfeld, it seems understandable that right from the beginning, a primary focus of Mennonite women's societies was the support of foreign missions. While it is not explicitly stated, it appears that the idea to form women's societies came from male church leaders, since they were the heads of churches; the fact that males led prayer and singing at women's society meetings indicates a certain degree of male involvement.

Not only did the spiritual awakening in Gnadenfeld prepare the ground for the establishment of Mennonite women's societies, it was also the context our of which the MB church originated. After signing a document of secession from the *Kirchliche* Mennonite (KM)[40] church in 1860, the MB church was formed; a church characterized by increased attention to Bible study, conversion, and moral living.[41] Women in the MB church seemed to have certain liberties to which they were previously unaccustomed in the KM church. These included:

> The emphasis on spontaneous conversion and antipathy toward tradition broke barriers and promoted equality in general, and also between the sexes. . . . With the introduction of Bible study, prayer meeting, Sunday school, and mission societies, a wide field was opened for Mennonite women. Now they could express their views in Bible studies, they participated audibly in prayer meetings, they taught Sunday-school classes, discussed missionary affairs in sewing circles and many other organizations, and as mission workers engaged in direct evangelism and teaching.[42]

They "organized meetings among themselves in which every member of the congregation, regardless of age or sex, as an equally qualified priest anointed with the Holy Spirit, explained the Scriptures and prayed aloud."[43]

Women in the MB church were also known to study theology alongside of men. For instance, it was during this time that Katharina Zacharias Martens, together with her husband, "pored over sermons and textbooks . . . they prepared to attend the highly esteemed Bielefeld School in Germany."[44] But, while it is true that when the MB church was first established, MB women were able to participate more freely in the church, we know that by the end of the century men held positions of authority and were the decision makers. Women "had no vote in church affairs, there was just *Bruderschaft*."[45] Women were Sunday school teachers and deaconesses. With a precedent set in the Netherlands, Mennonite women were active as deaconesses in Russia by the late 1800s.[46] A training institution, "Moria Society of Evangelical Sisters of Mercy" was established in 1909 in Halbstadt, Molotschna. Here single women could enrol in a three year nurses' training course as well as have their physical needs provided for, as long as they remained members of the Moria society.

Another role for women, already begun in Gnadenfeld, was the *Verein;*

by the late 1800s societies had been established within local Mennonite congregations. It is uncertain whether Mennonite women's societies continued from their origin in the 1840s in Gnadenfeld right through the late 1800s, but we know that by 1902 women's missionary circles existed in many villages.[47] In Gortchakov, a Schwestern Verein (Sisters' Society) was established before World War I.[48] In Davlekonovo, a cultural and economic centre of the Mennonite settlement in the Russian province of Ufa, both KM and MB Nähvereine (sewing societies) were established and a Yungfrauenverein (Young Women's Society) was organized between 1913 and 1916.[49]

In Russia, *Verein* meetings were held regularly in members' homes in order to work for missions.[50] Not only did Mennonite women sew, knit and crochet articles of clothing for missions; they also developed a worship ritual. In MB societies, "there would be singing, prayer, reading of Scripture, missionary reports. . . . Somebody would tell of her experience with the Lord or a poem. Coffee and *Zwieback* (rolls) would end the meeting."[51] The pattern was similar in KM societies. Sometimes called *Arbeitstunde* (work hour), women would work on quilts while one member read from a book.[52] Completed articles were later sold at an auction in the local school building, and the proceeds given to missions. In cities where women could walk to church, regular meetings were held in the church; but in rural areas, women did the work by themselves in their own homes, and assembled as a group only for the annual auction.[53]

As already noted in the establishment of women's societies in Gnadenfeld the reason for their existence seems to have been to contribute to the missionary effort. Catherine Klassen, a Canadian immigrant from Russia, notes that women's societies probably were first organized "when people became missionary minded."[54] While some members of *Vereine* went to foreign lands as missionaries, the vast majority of Mennonite women took on the role of support of missionaries through local church-based *Vereine*. The KM sent out their first missionaries in 1871 and the MB in 1885, when Abraham and Maria Friesen were sent to India.[55] In fact, Klassen refers to Abraham Friesen in her letter, stating that "mother's cousin Abraham Friesen was a missionary in India. When they reported back, there would be an incentive to have collections, support to give to missions."[56] According to her, *Vereine* were organized in the late 1800s out of a desire to support missions. This places the establishment of Mennonite women's societies in the context of the late nineteenth century enthusiasm for missions. Mennonite missionary activity did not happen in a vacuum. As indicated by historian John Webster Grant, there was a passion of the Christian church everywhere:

> Missionary enthusiasm inevitably overflowed the boundaries of Canada
> to claim a share in the effort to propagate Christianity throughout the
> world that was then engaging the interest of Christians everywhere.
> . . . Within a few decades there was a tremendous scattering of
> missionaries out of Christendom.[57]

Besides working for the cause of missions, Mennonite women's societies in Russia helped out in times of war. They made clothing, bandages, linen and bedding for victims of the Turkish War of 1877-1878 and the Russian-Japanese War of 1904.[58] During World War I, they knit scarves and mittens for men in the military;[59] in the village of Millerovo Mennonite women's groups organized for the care of wounded soldiers in a Mennonite owned flour mill.[60]

There is a striking similarity between components of women's gatherings and those of the larger church during the European period. Although there was no preaching as such in women's societies, most of the aspects of Sunday morning worship were included in Mennonite women's Verein meetings. In the Sunday morning church service in Russian Mennonite churches, this included combinations of preaching, teaching, prayer, reading from the Bible, and singing.[61] This was similar to what went on in women's society meetings. Thus, in Russia we already have a precedent for understanding women's societies as parallel church; an organization with the primary components of the larger institutional church.

Having considered the European context for Mennonite women's societies in Canada, it is useful to become familiar with the location of the major centres of settlement during the years of immigration, before moving on to discuss the establishment of *Vereine* in Canada.

In 1786, the first Mennonites to arrive in Upper Canada came from Pennsylvania just after the American Revolution. Of Swiss origin, these had emigrated from Europe to the United States about a hundred years prior. Russian Mennonites did not come to Canada until the latter part of the nineteenth century.

With the entry of Manitoba into Confederation in 1870, and the Manitoba School Act guaranteeing private schools, conditions were ripe for the settlement of approximately eight thousand Mennonites who left Russia for Manitoba between 1874 and 1880. The package offered by the Canadian government was appealing: exemption from military service; free land; freedom to educate their own children; the right to affirm, instead of swear, in taking an oath; and financial help for the voyage to Canada.[62] Several colonies of Mennonites—some of whom would later form the CMC—settled in Canada, and the MB migrated to the United States. Two reserves of land had been designated for the Mennonites in Manitoba. The largest group, originating from the Bergthal colony in Russia, settled on the East Reserve, just south of Winnipeg and east of the Red River. Villages on the East Reserve included Niverville, Blumenhort, Chortitz, Steinbach, Bergthal, and Grunthal. The next contingent of Mennonites from Russia, arriving in 1875, settled on the West Reserve in villages such as Winkler, Altona, Gretna, and Plum Coulee.

The subsequent movement of Mennonites form Manitoba westward was instigated by the decision of the provincial government in the 1880s to reorganize the reserves into municipalities. Seen as a threat to Mennonite culture and religion, the more conservative Mennonites (Old Colony) moved to Mexico while some of the more progressive group (Bergthaler) resettled in Saskatchewan and Alberta. In Saskatchewan, they joined the Rosenorter Mennonites who had arrived there from Russia in 1896. Out of a desire to maintain ties between the groups in Manitoba and Saskatchewan, the Conference of Mennonites in Central Canada (later called the CMC) was formed.

While the CMC was established by Mennonites who had immigrated directly to Canada from Russia, the arrival of the MB in Canada was due to expansion by American MB immigrants. They came to Canada as missionaries to Mennonites on the West Reserve in Manitoba which, in 1888, resulted in the establishment of the first Canadian MB congregation in Burwalde (now Winkler). Other MB churches were soon organized both in southern Manitoba and Saskatchewan.

By the time of the second major migration of Russian Mennonites to Canada (1923-1930), there already were CMC and MB settlements in Manitoba, Saskatchewan, and Alberta. New immigrants who came in the 1920s tended to settle in already established Mennonite communities, but this period also witnessed expansion into British Columbia and Ontario. At the same time, Mennonites were beginning to move to the cities seeking employment.

By 1940, CMC and MB communities had been established in Manitoba, Saskatchewan, Alberta, British Columbia, and Ontario. In Manitoba, major settlements were clustered in the Winkler/Altona area and Winnipeg. In northern Saskatchewan, Mennonites settled in places like Rosthern, Waldheim, Hepburn, Saskatoon, and Dalmeny; in the south, in towns such as Herbert, Main Centre, and Swift Current. In Alberta, key centres were Coaldale and Rosemary. In British Columbia, Mennonites settled in the Fraser Valley and Vancouver. In Ontario, they were concentrated in the Kitchener/Waterloo area, the Niagara Peninsula, and Leamington.

The third immigration of Mennonites to Canada began in 1947. Among them was a high percentage of widows and single women who tended to migrate to urban centres such as Vancouver, Kitchener/Waterloo, Winnipeg, and St. Catharines. By 1952 (the last year of the third immigration of Russian Mennonites to Canada), there were eighty CMC and 108 MB churches in Canada.[63] Mennonites were moving to the cities in larger numbers. Here they established retail businesses, religious educational institutions, health care facilities, and homes for the elderly. Along with this came a gradual acculturation to Canadian society, most obviously reflected in the gradual transition of the use of the German language of the English.

Throughout this period of time, as new churches were established, Mennonite women's societies were organized within them. These became a major avenue for Mennonite women to contribute to the missions program of the church, to receive encouragement and support from one another, and to be spiritually strengthened through their worship rituals.

Notes

1 J.C.Wenger, ed., *The Complete Writings of Menno Simons*, trans. Leonard Verduin (Scottdale: Herald Press, 1956).

2 Thieleman J. van Braght, *Martyrs' Mirror of the Defenseless Christians*, trans. Joseph F. Sohm (Lancaster County: N.P., 1837). The reliability of Van Braght's work has at times been questioned. Besides mistakes in recording names and dates of execution, some martyrs were omitted because the author did not want to include the Münsterites nor those who were anti-trinitarian. See Harold S. Bender and C. Henry Smith, eds., *Mennonite Encyclopedia*, 4 vols. (Scottdale: Mennonite Publishing House, 1955-57), 3:527. Since the particular errors and omissions discovered do not pertain to women's role in Anabaptism, there is no reason to suspect information which is pertinent to the present study.

3 Bender and Smith, eds., *Mennonite Encyclopedia*.

4 Menno Simons, "The True Christian Faith," in *The Complete Writings of Menno Simons*, pp. 343-91.

5 Ibid., p. 383.

6 Menno Simons, "Comforting Letter to a Widow," in *The Complete Writings of Menno Simons*, p. 1028.

7 "Sincere Appeal to Leonard Bouwen's Wife," in *The Complete Writings of Menno Simons*, p. 1038.

8 Bender and Smith, eds., *Mennonite Encyclopedia*, and Braght, *Martyrs' Mirror of the Defenseless Christians*, pp. 413-1100. I perused pages 413-1100 and examined every court record, story, and letter for indications of women's role within early Dutch Anabaptism.

9 Braght, *Martyrs' Mirror of the Defenseless Christians*, pp. 453, 668, 1080.

10 Ibid., p. 737.

11 A.L.E. Verheyden, *Anabaptism in Flanders, 1530-1650: A Century of Struggle* (Scottdale: Herald Press, 1961), p. 5.

12 Braght, *Martyrs' Mirror of the Defenseless Christians*, pp. 738, 842, 495, 522, 1092.

13 Ibid., pp. 495, 653, 481-482.

14 Ibid., p. 886.

15 Bender and Smith, eds., *Mennonite Encyclopedia*, 4:570.

16 Braght, *Martyrs' Mirror of the Defenseless Christians*, p. 711.

17 Ibid., p. 712.

18 Bender and Smith, eds., *Mennonite Encyclopedia*, 4:972 and Keith L. Sprunger, "God's Powerful Army of the Weak: Anabaptist Women of the Radical Reformation," in *Triumph Over Silence, Women in Protestant History*, Richard L. Greaves, ed. (Westport: Greenwood Press, 1985), p. 53.

19 Braght, *Martyrs' Mirror of the Defenseless Christians*, p. 481.

20 Bender and Smith, eds., *Mennonite Encyclopedia*, 1:19 and 4:973.

21 Ibid., 1:18-19.

22 Braght, *Martyrs' Mirror of the Defenseless Christians*, p. 551.

23 Marilyn French, *Beyond Power: On Women, Men, and Morals* (New York: Ballantine Books, 1985), p. 188.

24 Bender and Smith, eds., *Mennonite Encyclopedia*, 4:973.

25 Ibid., 2:22.

26 Ibid.

27 Menno Simons, "Foundation of Christian Doctrine," pp. 167, 200 and "Why I do not Cease Teaching and Writing," pp. 305-307 in *The Complete Writings of Menno Simons*.

28 Peter James Klassen, *The Economics of Anabaptism 1525-1560* (London: Mouton and Co., 1964), p. 43.

29 In the Netherlands during the 1500s, those Dutch Anabaptists who were affiliated with the teachings of Menno Simons were known as "Mennists". In Prussia, in the seventeenth and eighteenth centuries they were known as "Mennonit", and in Russia, from the nineteenth centuries it was replaced by "Mennonite". See Bender and Smith, eds., *Mennonite Encyclopedia*, 3:586-87.

30 Toews, *A History of the Mennonite Brethren Church*, p.13.

31 Peter M. Friesen, *The Mennonite Brotherhood in Russia (1789-1910)*, trans. and ed. J.B. Toews et al. (Fresno: General Conference of Mennonite Brethren Churches, 1978), p. 51.

32 Ibid., pp. 60, 68, 72.

33 Ibid., p. 51.

34 C. Henry Smith, *The Story of the Mennonites* (Newton: Mennonite Publication Office, 1950), p. 289.

35 James Urry, *None But Saints: The Transformation of Mennonite Life in Russia 1789-1889* (Winnipeg: Hyperion Press, 1989), pp. 56-57.

36 Bender and Smith, eds., *Mennonite Encyclopedia*, 2:531.

37 Jacob P. Bekker, *Origin of The Mennonite Brethren Church*, trans. D.E. Pauls and A.E. Janzen (Hillsboro: Mennonite Brethren Historical Society of the Midwest, 1973), pp. 25-26.

38 Bender and Smith, eds., *Mennonite Encyclopedia*, 2:531.

39 Bekker, *Origin of the Mennonite Brethren Church*, pp. 25-26.

40 After the separation of the MB from the established Mennonite church in Russia, the main body of Mennonites was designated *Kirchliche* (churchly) Mennonites. The CMC eventually became the largest Canadian Mennonite denomination of what were the *Kirchliche* Mennonites. Hereafter, the standard designation of *Kirchliche* Mennonites (KM) will be used when referring to these Mennonites in Russia..

41 Friesen, *The Mennonite Brotherhood in Russia*, pp. 230-232.

42 Bender and Smith, eds., *Mennonite Encyclopedia*, 4:973.

43 Friesen, *The Mennonite Brotherhood in Russia*, p. 377.

44 Hilda J. Born, "Plant Trees Wherever You Go: Katharina Zacharias Martens (1867-1929)," in *Women Among the Brethren*, p. 133.

45 Letter from Catherine Klassen, a leader within MB women's societies, Winnipeg, Manitoba, 25 April 25 1989.

46 Friesen, *The Mennonite Brotherhood in Russia*, p. 828.

47 Waldemar Janzen, "Foreign Mission Interest of the Mennonites in Russia Before World War I," *Mennonite Quarterly Review* 42, 1 (1968): 63.

48 Letter from Catherine Klassen.

49 Letter from Catherine Klassen; and Bender and Smith, eds., *Mennonite Encyclopedia*, 2:20.

50 Interview with Antonio and Benjamin Redekopp of Ste. Catherines, Ontario, 24 May 1989.

51 Letter from Catherine Klassen.

52 Interview with Katharine Langeman, Helen Peters, Hedie Wiens, Margaret Wiens, and Anna Fast of the George Street Senior Home of the Waterloo/Kitchener United Mennonite Church, Waterloo, Ontario, 19 March 1989.

53 Ibid.

54 Letter from Catherine Klassen.

55 Dyck, ed., *An Introduction to Mennonite History*, p. 136, and Toews, *A History of the Mennonite Brethren Church*, p. 99.

56 Letter from Catherine Klassen.

57 John Webster Grant, *The Church in the Canadian Era* (Burlington: Welch Publishing Company Inc., 1988), p. 55.

58 Friesen, *The Mennonite Brotherhood in Russia*, pp. 583-585, 830.

59 Letter from Catherine Klassen.

60 Interview with Antonio and Benjamin Redekopp.

61 Toews, *A History of the Mennonite Brethren Church*, pp. 57, 70 and Bekker, *Origin of the Mennonite Brethren Church*, p. 145.

62 The following sources were used for the historical sketch of Russian Mennonites in Canada: Peter F. Bargen, "The Coming of the Mennonites to Alberta," *Mennonite Life* 11, 2 (April 1956): 83-87; J.H. Enns, "City with Largest Mennonite Population: Winnipeg, Manitoba," *Mennonite Life* 11, 3 (July 1956): 112-114; Epp, *Mennonites in Canada*, 1786-1920, *Mennonites in Canada* 1920-1940, and *Mennonite Exodus: The Rescue and Resettlement of the Russian Mennonites Since the Communist Revolution*. (Altona: D.W. Friesen and Sns, 1962); J.H. Lohrenz, "The Mennonites in Winnipeg," *Mennonite Life* 6, 1 (January 1951): 16-25; Peter Paetkau and Lawrence Klippenstein, "Conference of Mennonites in Canada: Background and Origin," *Mennonite Life* 34, 4 (December 1979): 4-10; Toews, *A History of the Mennonite Brethren Church*; and B.B. Wiens, "Pioneering in British Columbia," *Mennonite Life* 1,2 (July 1946): 9-13.

63 Bender and Smith, eds., *Mennonite Encyclopedia*, 1: 671, and *1952 Yearbook of the Forty-Second Canadian Conference of the Mennonite Brethren Church of North America* (Winnipeg: The Christian Press, 1952), pp. 128-133.

PART TWO

Emergence and Establishment: 1874 - 1952

3

Why *Vereine*?

When Russian Mennonites immigrated to Canada, the institutional church was male dominated, and women's societies were considered subsidiary organizations. The CMC by-laws, written at the time of the incorporation of the CMC in 1947, referred to women's societies as subsidiary organizations and stated that these societies were answerable to the church for the nature of their activities, which "shall be in harmony with the constitution and aims of the conference."[1] The fact that they were called "subsidiary organizations" indicates their subordination to the institutional church. However, it appears that women did not object to the subsidiary status of their organizations; in the early years they even named their groups auxiliaries and aids.

The women's minimal role within the formal church structure in the early years in Canada is exemplified in the continued practice of *Bruderschaft*. The resolution of the 1879 MB General Conference of North America allowed for women to "take part in church activities as the Holy Spirit leads. However, they should not preach nor take part in discussion in business meetings of the church."[2] This was based on the conviction that, according to New Testament Pauline writings, especially 1Tim. 2:8-15, women should be silent in the church. The prevalence of male control within the church in the early years is recounted in one of the local congregation histories, which states that "like the majority of churches, the Whitewater Mennonite congregation was led strictly by men."[3] Gradually, local congregations gave women the vote. In at least two instances, it was a mission society that requested a voice for women. In 1949, the Naomi Mission Society of the First Mennonite Church in Saskatoon asked the church to grant women the right to vote, because, as they argued, while married women could have a voice through their husbands, widows and single women had no one to represent them at church business meetings.[4] A similar situation occurred in Kitchener/Waterloo in the early 1900s, when employed immigrant women requested the right to vote; the rationale was that since they contributed to the church treasury, they should be granted the vote.[5] It is difficult to determine how widespread this phenomenon was. More common, it seems, was the notion that men were supposed to run the church—an understanding among women in other Protestant denominations as well, who "felt no need to question the values of their own society concerning women . . . the members of the missionary societies did not consider themselves participants in the woman's movement."[6] Neither were members of Mennonite women's societies part of the women's movement. As one record of *Verein* activities states, "we find no mention of women's liberation."[7] For the most part, Mennonite women accepted the paradigm that men had certain responsibilities in the church and women had others; both were important. A past president of a women's society in Steinbach, Manitoba, states: "Even though the women work separately from the rest of the congregation, we still feel that we are very much a part of the whole . . . the women do their part and the men, theirs."[8] Specifically, women's work in the church was to raise money to support Mennonite missionaries overseas.

In the late 1880s, when Russian Mennonites began to immigrate to Canada, Mennonite women were not unique in their suppport of missions. By this time, Roman Catholic, Anglican, Methodist, and Presbyterian churches were already involved in fairly extensive overseas missions programs. Grant points out that

> among Protestants, women were the first to organize for the furtherance of the missionary cause and in Canada they have always been the chief instigators of enthusiasm for missions. . . . Such groups, although largely dependent on mite boxes and voluntary projects, raised astonishing sums for missionary purposes.[9]

During this time, two kinds of Protestant women's groups were organized: missionary societies that concerned themselves with raising funds to support missionaries, and ladies aids that assisted with local church needs. The first local women's missionary association established in Canada was by Presbyterian women on Prince Edward Island in 1825,[10] and by the 1880s, a number of Protestant women's societies had organized nationally. Alongside of missionary societies in local congregations, ladies aid societies were also established. These assisted in the affairs of the local church, such as supplying furnishings, paying for repairs, and visiting the sick. By the 1890s, there were 1,350 ladies aid societies in Canadian Methodist churches alone.[11] At this time, Mennonite women were also busy organizing their own societies.

As more and more Russian Mennonites immigrated to Canada and new Mennonite churches were established, Mennonite women's societies were formed within them, sometimes initiated by Mennonite men and other times by women. Organization of women's groups by male church leaders was a common phenomenon in Protestant traditions. The Woman's Missionary Society of the Methodist Church, for example, was established in Ontario when, in 1880, Rev. A. Sutherland, a Methodist minister, "pleaded the need of woman's energy in mission work."[12] Similarly, in 1876, the Foreign Missions Committee of the Presbyterian Church initiated the organization of the Women's Foreign Missionary Society, when "two leading churchmen, Rev. Dr. William MacLaren and Rev. Dr. Alexander Topp, conveyed the Foreign Mission Committee's desire that such a society be organized."[13] It is not surprising that in the first decades of Mennonites in Canada, numerous Mennonite women's societies were also started by men. In 1915, a women's society was formed in Drake, Saskatchewan, when Rev. Mike Horsch from the CMC mission board asked women to sew clothing for a mission station.[14] Another was instigated by a pastor in Eigenheim, Saskatchewan, who suggested that women organize a

Nähverein.[15] In Herbert, Saskatchewan, a women's group was initiated by a male missionary who pleaded for funds for missions in India.[16] In Crystal City, Manitoba, a ladies aid was organized when C.F. Klassen reported on the plight of refugees in Europe.[17] In Osler, Saskatchewan, during a Sunday morning church service in 1949, the minister of the church "invited all interested ladies to rise and thus indicate they were willing to further God's work,"[18] and a women's society was established right there and then. In these cases, male church leaders saw needs which they felt would be appropriate for women to fulfil. Women were asked to participate in the cause of missions by sewing, an activity viewed as suitable for women. Women seemed pleased to participate in the work of the church in this way.

While some women's societies in Protestant traditions were initiated by men, others were organized by women. For instance, the first missionary society of the Baptist church was established in 1870 by Hannah Maria Norris who, although she felt called by God to be a missionary, was refused financial support of the Mission Board, so she asked women to support her.[19] That year she organized thirty-three "circles" in her home province of New Brunswick for her own missionary support.[20] Likewise, some Mennonite women's societies were initiated by women. For example, in 1929, when a woman in a Mennonite church in Meadow Lake, Saskatchewan, realized that women did not have a significant role within the already established programs of the church, asked the question: "Why could not we women get together, and get some kind of ladies aid or sewing circle going and get busy doing something in an organized way?"[21] As a result, a women's society began in that church. A similar incident occurred in Sardis, British Columbia, in 1930, when "coming from the Sunday morning service, Mrs. Katharina Friesen (wife of Rev. B.B. Friesen) felt a burden on her heart. What could they do to get their own church? . . . Could they organize a sewing circle and start raising money for this project?"[22] In this instance, there was a need for a church building and a woman decided to form a woman's society to raise money to meet that need.

Whether instigated by women or men, most *Vereine* were organized in order to meet a particular need, either locally or in other countries where Mennonite missionaries were working. But what was the motivation for their involvement? What motivated them to serve as they did?

Wendy Mitchinson has noted that women formed missionary societies because "they believed that they had a direct command from God to spread his gospel."[23] Their impetus was a faith experience based on biblical reflection. This was certainly the case in Mennonite women's societies; Mennonite women were clear about their biblical motivation.

Mennonite women's work of service was inspired by biblical teaching. "Love to God" was the reason for the organization of the first women's group of the Clearbrook MB Church.[24] In 1936, the Naomi-Ruth *Verein* of the First United Mennonite Church in Vancouver expressed their service in this way:

"With God's help, we too, even if we are few in numbers, want to try to add our coins to help build the Kingdom of Heaven."[25] In Altona, Manitoba, the Mary Martha Mission Group situated the work of their group within a long tradition of Christian women who had served God: "Since the beginning of Christianity, women have had their own special role to play in the service of the Master. Much of it was lowly work, perhaps, but they did not consider it so for they were serving the One they loved."[26]

That Mennonite women were motivated by a call of God to service is evident by the biblical texts they chose as mottos for their groups. These included the following:

> And let us not be weary in well doing: for in due season we shall reap, if we faint not. As we have therefore opportunity, let us do good unto all men,[27] especially unto them who are of the household of faith. (Gal. 6:9,10)
>
> Now there was at Joppa a certain disciple named Tabitha, which by interpretation is called Dorcas: this woman was full of good works and almsdeeds which she did. (Acts 9:36)
>
> And whatsoever ye do, in word or deed, do all in the name of the Lord Jesus, giving thanks to God the Father by him. (Col. 3:17)
>
> Therefore all things whatsoever ye would that men should do to you, do ye even so to them: for this is the law and the prophets. (Matt. 7:12)
>
> Bear ye one another's burdens, and so fulfil the law of Christ. (Gal. 6:2)
>
> Let him that stole steal no more: but rather let him labour, working with his hands the thing which is good, that he may have to give to him that needeth. (Eph. 4:28)
>
> I must work the works of him (Jesus) that sent me while it is day; night cometh when no man can work. (Jn. 9:4)
>
> But let every man prove his own work, and then shall he have rejoicing in himself alone, and not in another. (Gal. 6:4)
>
> Pray ye therefore the Lord of the harvest, that he will send forth labourers into his harvest. (Matt. 9:38)

The choice of texts such as these for group mottos shows that the emphasis on service had its basis in biblical texts. Texts chosen by Mennonite women have to do with doing good deeds, working with one's hands, and giving to those in need. Mennonite women viewed their work for missions as done directly for God. They were doing "the works of him (Jesus)."

Besides choosing biblical texts as mottos, women often called their societies by names of women in the Bible, such as Tabitha, Naomi, Ruth, Salome, Lydia, Mary, and Martha. It appears that identification with these women was strong enough for Mennonite women to name their societies after them.

Whereas Mennonite women were clear about the purpose of their *Verein*, Mennonite men, often questioning their motivation, were known to refer to women's societies as gossip centres. Such male criticism of *Vereine* is evident, for example, in this segment of a poem written in the late 1940s:

> Why do they sew so much?
> It's just to pass the time,
> They only gossip and turn their heads.[28]

The Ebenezer Ladies Aid in Steinbach, Manitoba, was also aware of this perception of women's groups. They reflected that

> sometimes the Ladies Aids are ridiculed and sarcastically spoken of as being mere "coffee-klatsches" but that is not true of our congregation. Neither is that remark deserving of any LadiesAid . . . The field of service for everyone, but especially for the women, is very big and no doubt the future will offer many opportunities of service for which God may grant us willing hands and hearts.[29]

In the 1930s, *Vereine* also came under criticism in the church periodical, *Mennonitische Rundschau*, and was subsequently defended by a member of a *Verein*, who wrote that not one *Verein* deserved to be thought of as self righteous.[30] Against accusations such as these, Mennonite women affirmed their biblical motivation for service through participation in church women's societies.

In the era of the establishment of Mennonite women's societies, societies became a context for Mennonite women to live out their identity as Christian women in a way that was considered appropriate by both themselves and the institutional church. Restricted in their roles within the larger church institution, here they could answer the call of God by raising money for missions through the work of their own hands (knitting and sewing). That the formation of their societies was biblically based is evident both in the biblical texts that were chosen as mottos for their groups as well as the names by which groups were identified.

Notes

1 "Bill C. An Act to Incorporate Conference of Mennonites in Canada," in *Konferenz* (Coaldale: Conference of Mennonites in Canada, 1947), p. 40.

2 *General Conference Yearbook*, 1879, p. 4. It should be noted that some Canadian Mennonite Brethren churches decided not to adhere to this resolution and allowed women to attend church business meetings.

3 Henry Albrecht et al., *History of the Whitewater Mennonite Church Boissevain, Manitoba 1927-1987* (Boissevain: Whitewater Mennonite Church, 1987), p. 86.

4 Esther Patkau, ed., *First Mennonite Church in Saskatoon 1923-1982* (Saskatoon: First Mennonite Church, 1982), p. 104.

5 Interviews with Katherine Langeman, Helen Peters, Hedie Wiens, Margaret Wiens, and Anna Fast.

6 Mitchinson, "Canadian Women and Church Missionary Societies in the Nineteenth Century," p. 73.

7 H.T. Klassen, *Birth and Growth of the Eigenheim Mennonite Church 1892-1974* (Rosthern: Eigenheim Mennonite Church, 1974), p. 9.

8 Nettie Neufeld and Jessie Peters, *Fifty Years Ebenezer Verein 1936-1986* (Steinbach: Ebenezer *Verein*, 1987), p. 14.

9   Grant, *The Church in the Canadian Era*, 1988, p. 57.

10 Mitchinson, "Canadian Women and Church Missionary Societies in the Nineteenth Century," p. 61.

11 Nancy Hall, "The Professionalisation of Women Workers in the Methodist, Presbyterian, and United Churches of Canada," in *First Days Fighting Days: Women in Manitoba History*, ed. Mary Kinnear (Regina: Canadian Plains Research Center, 1987), p. 122.

12 Graham, *Forty-Five Years Effort of the Woman's Missionary Society*, p. 4.

13 Margaret E. McPherson, "Head, heart and purse: The Presbyterian Women's Missionary Society in Canada, 1876-1925," in *Prairie Spirit: Perspectives on the Heritage of the United Church of Canada in the West*, ed. Dennis L. Butcher et al. (Winnipeg: University of Manitoba Press, 1985), p. 151.

14 Bartel, *Saskatchewan Women in Mission*, p. 17.

15 Ibid., p. 26.

16 Ibid., p. 38.

17 Froese, *Manitoba Mennonite Women in Mission*, p. 27.

18 Bartel, *Saskatchewan Women in Mission*, p. 54.

19 Merrick, *These Impossible Women*, p. 19.

20 Ibid.

21 Bartel, *Saskatchewan Women in Mission*, p. 50.

22 *A History of the First Mennonite Church Greendale B.C.* (Greendale: First Mennonite Church, 1976), p. 8.

23 Mitchinson, "Canadian Women and Church Missionary Societies in the Nineteenth Century," p. 73.

24 Louise Enns, "Ladies fellowship groups, Clearbrook MB Church," *History of the Clearbrook MB Church: 1936-1986*, (N.p., 1986), p. 97.

25 Rempel, *History of B.C. Mennonite Women in Mission*, p. 74. The reference to "coins" probably refers to Jesus' observation that the woman who dropped two "mites" into the temple treasury gave more than the wealthy because she gave all she had. More than likely, this inspired the Naomi-Ruth *Verein* to think they could make a difference with their contributions.

26 Froese, *Manitoba Mennonite Women in Mission*, p. 16.

27 Texts are from the King James Version of the Bible since this was the version used in Mennonite churches at this time. The language of the King James Version is not inclusive.

28 Heinz Janzen, *Gedicht* [Poem], a poem about donations by Mennonite women's societies of the Waterloo-Kitchener Mennonite Church to replace the church roof, Waterloo, Ontario, late 1940s.

29 Neufeld and Peters, *Fifty Years Ebenezer Verein*, p. 14-15.

30 See "*Frauenvereinsarbeit*," *Mennonitische Rundschau* (7 März 1934):5 and "*An die Frauenvereine!*" *Mennonitische Rundschau* (16 Januar 1935):6.

4

Service, Fellowship and Worship

While the most obvious focus for Mennonite women's societies was service, women also organized societies for the purpose of, in their words, "fellowship." In their regularly held gatherings, they supported one another in difficult times. Meetings also provided an occasion for spiritual strengthening in the worship times which customarily were part of their time together. The three foci of service, fellowship, and worship were primary for Mennonite women's societies.

Through their societies, Mennonite women supported the programs of the church, at home and abroad. They often supported a number of projects at once, as is illustrated in the list of projects recorded in the 1925 minutes of a Mennonite women's group in Aberdeen, Saskatchewan:

> the buying of medicines for a sick child or adult; articles of clothing and food for a poor family; glasses for several people, and other such like. Monies to other countries went to Russia, Germany, India and Africa. *"Biblische Geschichte"* (Bible stories) were bought for the Sunday School, recitation books for the *Jugenverein* (youth society) and subsequent needs of our local church.[1]

In some instances, Mennonite women's societies contributed funds for the construction of a church building.[2] For example, in 1940, the Ladies Fellowship of the Clearbrook MB Church raised the entire amount needed for the material for the first church sanctuary.[3]

Mennonite male leaders often suggested projects for women's societies to support. In 1943, at the occasion of the organization of the CMC Saskatchewan Women in Mission, Rev. J.J. Thiessen suggested that their first project be the Margaret Toews Scholarship.[4] They followed his advice. Likewise, at the request of Rev. Mike Horsch, the CMC *Nähverein* in Drake, Saskatchewan, sewed clothing for the needy in Montana.[5] MB women's societies generally became aware of mission projects through the Board of Foreign Missions of North America. In fact, this male-controlled board of missions considered Mennonite women's societies "a channel through which the Board of Foreign Missions and missionaries could make their needs known."[6]

While in these and other instances, selection of projects was made by males or by a male-dominated board, there were exceptions. Some societies, as they became aware of needs, chose whatever mission projects they wished to support. For example, the Zoar Ladies Aid of Waldheim, Saskatchewan, "made and sent layettes and print dresses for children. On July 12, 1917, we made a direct offering to missionary Penners in India toward the buying of a cow."[7] That they had a certain amount of direct communication with missionaries is evident by the fact that, during meetings of Mennonite women's societies, letters from missionaries would often be read. Later, Mennonite women's societies received ideas for projects from MCC (Mennonite Central Committee)[8] and from their own provincial organizations which, among CMC women's societies, began to be established in the late 1930s.[9]

By far, the most important area of service for Mennonite women in the early years was the support of foreign missions through the sale of their own handwork. In some cases, this involved sending clothing directly to missionaries, but the most common method to support the mission effort was to sew, knit or crochet articles to be sold at annual missions' auction sales, the proceeds of which would be sent to support mission projects. In the early years, societies collected small amounts of money from their members and purchased fabric remnants from Eaton's catalogue, which were then sewed into articles to be auctioned.[10] As in other Protestant traditions, the annual mission sale became a common way for women across Canada to sell articles they had sewn and knit during the year.[11]

Just as Mennonite women's societies had been dependent on male mission boards to alert them to projects they could support, they were also likely to process their funds through these same mission boards. For example, the history of CMC Women in Mission indicates that in the late 1920s in Southwestern Ontario, money from mission sales "was passed on to the men who gave it to worthy charities."[12] While this method was common, societies also sent money directly to missionaries in the early 1900s.[13] Later, after women's organizations were established provincially, local women's groups channelled money through their own provincial organizations.[14]

In addition to supporting Mennonite missions and local churches, Mennonite women were quick to respond to other needs of which they became aware. During World War I, knitting and sewing were done at the request of the Red Cross, as in the case of the Ladies Aid of Aberdeen who "were asked by the Rosthern Branch (of the Red Cross) to knit and sew for the men overseas."[15] Women participated in a similar way during World War II: "During the war years the women also did a lot of sewing and knitting for the Red Cross. Many boxes of yarn were brought to the church to be divided among the sisters and worked into hats, scarves, mitts, gloves and socks in varying sizes."[16] During the depression of the 1930s, Mennonite women's societies gave food and clothing to families in their communities.[17]

It is evident that service was central for Mennonite women's societies by the names they chose to identify their groups. The act of naming their societies was not unique to Mennonite women; women in other Protestant denominations also gave names to their organizations. Common names for groups that were organized to support missions among Methodist, Presbyterian, Church of England, and Baptist women included Missionary Society, Foreign Missionary Society, or Home Missionary Society. Those established in order to support local church needs were called ladies aids.[18] One exception was among

Methodist groups in which Dorcas societies were organized to care for the sick and poor. Similarly, names of Mennonite women's societies expressed the groups' function, with one obvious difference: there was no differentiation between missionary societies and aids. Generally, most Mennonite societies, whether they were called mission societies or ladies aids, attended both to foreign missions and local church needs. Another difference between the naming of Mennonite women's societies and that of other Protestant women's groups was that there was a greater variety of names among Mennonite women's societies. (See tables 2 and 3 for variety and percentage distribution of names exemplifying similar foci.)

Names denoting aid/help/service comprised 37 percent of CMC names and 22.5 percent of MB names. When considering all names that imply a service orientation (names referring to missions, sewing, aid, help, or service), 70.5 percent of CMC names and 65 percent of MB names are included. Not as common were names signifying fellowship: only 15 percent of MB groups and 2.5 percent of CMC groups. But that does not mean that fellowship was not an important aspect of women's purpose for gathering. Because of the isolation they felt in the early years, women felt the need to communicate with other women. This was so, whether they were Mennonite, Presbyterian, Methodist, or Baptist: "women hungered for the companionship of their sisters . . . for fellowship was so necessary in those early days when distances were travelled by foot."[19] The importance of fellowship for Mennonite women is illustrated in the meaning which the women of the South Western Ontario Women in Mission attributed to the word *Verein*:

> Literally translated the word *Verein* means a union, society, or club. However, to the women in the *Verein*, the word has come to mean much more. As we know it, it is a group that works together for a common goal, yes, but it is also a group whose members give each other friendship and support as they experience the various stages of their lives and the joys and struggles they bring.[20]

An account of the first Mennonite sewing circle in Port Rowan, Ontario, in 1926, explicitly states that the group organized for the sake of fellowship. As new immigrants to Canada, "a feeling of loneliness is often experienced when one moves to a new country with a foreign language, and as a result of this a deep need for fellowship with those of your own kind develops. . . . Out of this need arose the formation, in those early years, of the *Kränzchen*."[21] As the following recollections show, sharing with other women was of great benefit to these pioneer women:

> The earliest record of minutes we have are from 1924. . . . Bearing in mind that much of the travelling was done by horse and buggy, or sleigh, it really was a day off. . . . This, of course, meant that they were at your house for dinner as well as *faspa* (an evening meal of rolls, cheese, and cake). But knowing women, once they had the idea, any

Table 2
Percentage Distribution of Names of CMC Women's Societies
1874-1952

CATEGORY	NAMES	TOTAL	PERCENTAGE
Missions	Junior Ladies Mission Society, *Missionsverein* (3x), Marissa Mission Group, Women in Mission (2x), Women's Missionary Society (2x), The Missionary Circle, Mission Helpers, Women's Mission Society, Missions *Frauenverein*, Ladies Mission Club, Missionary Society, Mission Workers	16	13.0
Sewing	Sewing Circle (6x), *Nähverein* (8x), *Abendkränzchen, Edelweisskränzchen, Kränzchen* (3x), Girls' Sewing Club, *Frauen Nähverein*	21	17.0
Aid/Help/Service	Ladies Aid (22x), Senior Ladies Aid (6x), Junior Aid (2x), Willing Helpers (3x), *Hilfsverein, Willigen Hände, Verein Helfende Hände, Wohltätigkeitsverein,* Willing Helpers Ladies Aid, Busy Bees Circle, Merry Co-Workers Club, Goodwill Society, Goodwill Ladies Aid, Women's Auxiliary, Ladies Auxiliary	44	37.0
Missions & Aid	Mission Ladies Aid	1	1.0
Missions & Biblical Woman's Name	Tabitha Mission Society, Mary Martha Mission Group, *Tabea Missionsverein*	3	2.5
Biblical Woman's Name	*Maria-Martha Verein* (3x), Dorcas Circle, Lydia *Verein, Tabea Verein* (2x), Tabithian Followers	8	7.0
Fellowship	*Gemeinde Verein,* Ladies Fellowship, Women's Christian Fellowship	3	2.5
Other	*Frauenverein* (7x), *Schnetke Conference, Mädchen Verein, Stadt's Verein, Verein* (10x), *Sonnenstrahl Verein,* Friendly Hour, Young Women's Club, Younger Group	24	20.0[22]
Total		120	100

Translations for German names are as follows: *Missionsverein* (Mission Society), *Frauenverein* (Women's Society), *Nähverein* (Sewing Society), *Abendkränzchen* (Evening Sewing Circle), *Edelweisskränzchen* (Edelweiss Sewing Society), *Kränzchen* (Sewing Society), *Frauen Nähverein* (Women's Sewing Society), *Hilfsverein* (Helping Society), *Willigen Hände* (Willing Hands), *Verein Helfende Hände* (Helping Hands Society), *Wohltätigkeitsverein* (a society which extends charity), *Tabea Missionsverein* (Tabitha Missions Society), *Gemeinde Verein* (Fellowship Society), *Schnetke Conference* (a conference with a variety of components), *Mädchen Verein* (Girls' Society), *Stadt's Verein* (Town Society), and *Sonnenstrahl Verein*

(Sunbeam Society). The word *Kränzchen* literally means "a party", but women translate it "sewing circle."

Table 3
Percentage Distribution of Names of MB Women's Societies[23]
1874-1952

CATEGORY	NAMES	TOTAL	PERCENTAGE
Missions	*Missionsverein* (3x), Young Ladies Mission Group, Women's Missionary Service, Mission Group	6	15.0
Sewing	*Nähverein* (3x), *Schwestern Nähverein*, *Blumenkränzchen*, *Kränzchen*, Sunshine Sewing Circle	7	17.5
Missions & Sewing	*Missionskränzchen* (2x), Missions *Nähverein*	3	7.5
Aid/Help/Service	Ladies Aid (3x), Junior Ladies Aid, Senior Ladies Aid (2x), Willing Workers Aid Society, Willing Helpers Club, Christian Service Club	9	22.5
Missions & Fellowship	Ladies Missionary Fellowship	1	2.5
Biblical Woman's Name	*Tabea Verein* (2x), *Salome Verein*	3	7.5
Fellowship	Ladies Fellowship (2x), Ladies Christian Fellowship, Women's Christian Fellowship	4	10.0
Biblical Woman's Name & Fellowship	Mary Martha Fellowship	1	2.5
Other	*Verein*, *Frauenverein* (3x), *Jung Frauen Verein*, *Schwestern Verein*	6	15.0
Total		40	100

Translations for German names not already translated are as follows: *Schwestern Nähverein* (Sisters' Sewing Society), *Blumenkränzchen* (Flowers Sewing Society), *Missionskränzchen* (Mission Sewing Society), *Salome Verein* (Salome Society), *Jung Frauen Verein* (Young Women's Society), and *Schwesternverein* (Sisters' Society).

> sacrifices made were not too much to ask, and the end result was the more blessed, and life more enjoyable for having been together and shared.[24]
>
> As far back as I can remember the ladies have gathered together to have fellowship. We ladies seem to have a greater need to share our joys and sorrows, our ups and downs than the men have.[25]

It is not only an organization to do good work and support missions, but
for the woman the Ladies Aid has great personal value. Once or twice
a month she frees herself from her household tasks and gets together
with her sisters. She leaves her troubles at home, shares with her fellow
sisters and then arrives back home refreshed.[26]

The fellowship and support women experienced was not the only
personal benefit, however, that women received in their regular meetings. Just
as important to them was the spiritual nourishment they obtained through their
worship rituals. The religious aspect of the *Vereine* meetings, sometimes
referred to as Christian or spiritual fellowship,[27] was a common component of
their gathering. Women's groups in the Leamington MB Church reported that
"meetings always had a strong spiritual emphasis with different sisters taking part
in scripture reading, devotionals and prayers and singing our favourite hymns."[28]
Members of a *Verein* in Winnipeg in the late 1920s wrote about it in this way:

On Thursdays we are drawn to the *Verein* where we sing, read and pray
and often voluntary recitations are presented. Then we depart feeling
blessed and renewed.

The evenings at the *Verein* are always hours of blessing for us. Many
a girl arrives tired, discouraged, in need of comfort and hungry but she
leaves the church refreshed by food from heaven, courageously
determined to follow the way He leads, to work and to serve in the
strength of the Lord.[29]

Early on, women developed a specific worship pattern for their meetings.
Commonly, meetings began with Bible reading, prayer, and singing.[30] As in
other Protestant women's societies in the early 1900s, men would often be the
ones to open women's meetings with Bible reading and prayer and to close
meetings with prayer.[31] In one Mennonite society, the male minister was in
attendance for society elections and he was also treasurer of the group.[32] To
some degree, men's involvement was a matter of convenience, since men would
often drive their wives to *Verein* meetings and stay in another room of the house
until the women's meetings were over. This meant that men were already there
and could open women's meetings with Bible reading and prayer, although it
appears that sometimes ministers were invited specifically for this purpose, as
indicated in the following account of the Hochfeld Sewing Circle in the Hague
Mennonite Church:

Our meetings took place every second week, and since this always
entailed driving, the husbands of the members were present also, as
were the ministers. Our meetings were opened by singing, scripture
reading and prayer. This was generally done by one of the ministers.[33]

There is no indication that women objected to this practice, but it changed
gradually until women took responsibility themselves for every aspect of their
meetings. For instance, by the late 1940s, Mennonite women in the Mennonite
Ladies Aid of Gem, Alberta, began to take charge themselves of the opening of
their meetings.[34]

While men sometimes opened and closed women's meetings, women took charge of the rest of their time together. This often consisted of a Bible study or devotional, discussion of business, and an offering of money. Sometimes, women would work on their handwork for a portion of the meeting while one member read from a devotional book or the Bible. In one instance, books read included *Women of the Old Testament* and *Women of the New Testament*.[35] Meetings generally closed with prayer and eating together. Women have described their worship ritual in the following ways:

> When the first Ladies Aid started in Greendale the ladies met in the homes. They would open the meetings with a short Bible study and prayer. Then one of the ladies would read an interesting spiritual book or portion of Scripture while the rest of the ladies did handwork. The meeting was closed with song and prayer. An offering was taken and refreshments were served most of the time.[36]

> Song, scripture and prayer opened the meeting, a Bible verse was quoted by each member, the business was discussed and then each took up some needlework. All members united to pray the Lord's prayer at the close and then a fellowship *Faspa* followed.[37]

It is understandable that components of the worship time in Mennonite women's societies were strikingly similar to the elements of worship in weekly Mennonite church services. Mennonite women learned about worship from the church, where services included prayer, scripture reading, singing, an offering, and the sermon(s). Periodically the Lord's supper (the Eucharist) was shared. Such a close similarity between the components of the Sunday church service and that of women's society meetings raises the possibility that the women's society functioned as a parallel church for Mennonite women. One major difference between the two was that the church worship was male led, while the women's society meeting was, for the most part, female planned and led. The women's society became a context in which women could determine how their spiritual needs would be met. They could study the Bible for themselves, decide which songs they would sing, and choose which religious books they would read. While for the most part Mennonite women accepted their role in the larger church institution, they made up for it in their own *Verein* meetings, in which, *de facto*, they conducted their own church.

Notes

1 Bartel, *Saskatchewan Women in Mission*, p. 12.

2 *A History of the First Mennonite Church Greendale B.C.*, p. 8; and Rempel, ed., *History of B.C. Mennonite Women in Mission*, p. 23.

3 *History of the Clearbrook MB Church: 1936-1986*, p. 97.

4 Bartel, *Saskatchewan Women in Mission*, p. 1.

5 "Report of the North Star Senior Ladies Aid," North Star Mennonite Church, Drake, Saskatchewan, n.d.

6   Walter Wiebe, ed., *A Century of Grace and Witness (1860-1960)* (Hillsboro: Mennonite Brethren Publishing House, 1960), p. 72. This was further corroborated in a class on MB history at the Mennonite Brethren Biblical Seminary in 1981 offered by J.B. Toews, who had been General Secretary of the MB Board of Missions in the late 1950s. He reported that when a financial crisis arose, he would send word to all MB women's societies instead of church pastors, because he found that women's groups responded more quickly.

7   Bartel, *Saskatchewan Women in Mission*, p. 86.

8   Mennonite Central Committee, a relief and service agency supported by most North American Mennonites, was established in 1920. See Bender and Smith, eds., *The Mennonite Encyclopedia*, 3:605.

9   N.N. Driedger, *The Leamington United Mennonite Church: Establishment and Development 1925-1972* (Altona: D.W. Friesen and Sons, 1972), p. 124, and *The Niagara United Mennonite Church 1938-1988*, (Niagara: Niagara United Mennonite Church, 1988), p. 84. In the CMC, British Columbia women were the first to organize provincially in 1939, and Alberta women were the last in 1948. Women in the MB church did not organize provincially until the late 1950s.

10 *A History of the First Mennonite Church Greendale B.C.*, p. 9.

11 National Council of Women of Canada, *Women of Canada, Their Life and Work* (N.p.: National Council of Women of Canada, 1900; reprint ed., 1956), p. 298.

12 Toews, ed., *South Western Ontario Women in Mission*, p. 11.

13 *Leamington Mennonite Brethren Church*, p. 86.

14 Neufeld, ed., *History of Alberta Mennonite Women in Mission*, pp. 9, 73.

15 Bartel, *Saskatchewan Women in Mission*, p. 12.

16 *Leamington Mennonite Brethren Church*, p. 38.

17 Bartel, *Saskatchewan Women in Mission*, p. 62.

18 National Council of Women of Canada, *Women of Canada, Their Life and Work*, pp. 303, 305, 307, 309.

19 Davy, Project Coordinator, *Women, Work and Worship*, p. 18.

20 Toews, ed., *South Western Ontario Women in Mission*, p. 5.

21 David Teigrob, *What Mean These Stones? Mennonite Brethren Church Port Rowan (1927-1977)* (St. Catharines: Knight Publishing and Lincoln Graphics, 1979), p. 78.

22 The high percentage in the "Other" category is due to the fact that each of the ten groups were simply called *Verein*.

23 There are fewer names for MB women's societies because of the lack of source material on the early years of MB women's societies.

24 Bartel, *Saskatchewan Women in Mission*, p. 12.

25 Mary Pauls, "The Arnaud Mennonite Brethren Ladies' Fellowship," in *Arnaud Through the Years*, ed. Christine M. Nichols (Steinbach: Derksen Printers, 1974), p. 75.

26 Neufeld and Peters, *Fifty Years Ebenezer Verein*, p. 13.

27 Esther (Bergman) Rempel, "Ladies Aid," in *Borden Mennonite Brethren Church: Precious Memories (1905-1980)*, ed. Orla Block (N.p.: n.d.), p. 41.

28 *Leamington Mennonite Brethren Church*, p. 38.

29 Thiessen, *The City Mission in Winnipeg*, pp. 90-91. This *Verein* was in one of the girls' homes established to house immigrant Mennonite girls who went to the city to work as domestics. The link between girls who were part of *Vereine* in these homes and those who later became leaders of *Vereine* in local churches is not addressed in this book.

30 Katherine Harder, ed., *The Greendale Mennonite Brethren Church (1931-1981)* (Cloverdale: Greendale Mennonite Brethren Church, 1981), pp. 166-67.

31 Froese, *Manitoba Mennonite Women in Mission*, pp. 44, 59, and Bartel, *Saskatchewan Women in Mission*, pp. 53, 79.

32 *Mennonite Church Rosemary* (Altona: D.W. Friesen and Sons, 1980), p. 51.

33 Helena Friesen, "The Hochfeld Sewing Circle," in *A History of the Hague Mennonite Church, Hague, Saskatchewan 1900-1975*, ed. John D. Rempel (Rosthern: Hague Mennonite Church, 1975), p. 59.

34 Neufeld, ed., *History of the Alberta Mennonite Women in Mission*, p. 85.

35 John D. Rempel, *A History of the Hague Mennonite Church, Hague Saskatchewan 1900-1975* (Rosthern: Hague Mennonite Church, 1975), p. 59.

36 Harder, ed., *The Greendale Mennonite Brethren Church*, pp. 166-67.

37 Bartel, *Saskatchewan Women in Mission*, p. 39.

PART THREE

Growth and Development: 1953-1969

5

Roles of Mennonite Women in Church and Home

In the 1950s there was an increased emphasis in Canadian society on women's place in the home.[1] Churches also emphasized the importance of women's role as mothers. At a time when Mennonite women's primary role was that of homemaker, they were also limited in the institutional church. Because of this, increasingly they may have viewed their societies as their primary outlet for service as well as an opportunity for spiritual expression and regular fellowship with other women. Perhaps this is one reason why Mennonite women's societies were at their peak between 1953 and 1969.

The phenomenon of restricting women's roles in the church was not unique to Mennonite communities. Even in the United Church of Canada, where women had been ordained since 1936, an article written in a 1963 church periodical encouraged women to work for the church in roles other than pastoral leadership, roles such as "Christian education, social service, teaching, nursing, evangelism and other educational fields."[2] In both CMC and MB traditions, women were encouraged to take subordinate, supportive roles. In a 1962 editorial of *The Canadian Mennonite*, CMC church secretaries were portrayed as modern deaconesses in a support role to church pastors who "make possible the work of many modern apostles."[3] Appealing to biblical texts, church leaders urged women to take their place subordinate to men. In 1963, I.W. Redekopp, in "The Woman's Place in the Church," differentiated between 'service' and 'position' of women. Referring to Gal. 3:28 and to specific women who were teachers, prophetesses, and deaconesses (Acts 1:14; 12:2; 16:1,14; 18:26; 21:8,9), he encouraged women to use their gifts in the service of the church. On the other hand, on the basis of Pauline texts (1 Cor. 12:12-14; 14:34; 1 Tim. 2:12; Tit. 2:3-5), he concluded that women should be submissive, since "it is a woman's gift to serve through submission. The desire to be led is in her nature. If she grasps for leadership she leaves her greatest gift."[4] Thus, concluded Redekopp, singing, mission work, and teaching women and children were appropriate areas of service for women, "as long as it is not done in such a way as to set herself up as an authority over man in the church."[5]

In 1966, New Testament MB scholar David Ewert affirmed a service role for women and maintained that the subordination of women was biblical. Quoting from 1 Timothy 2 and 1 Corinthians 14, he claimed that the principle of subordination was "inherent in the order of creation" and that "if the practice of the early church is to be our guide, then women should not lead in any way in public worship, whether in preaching or praying."[6] Although the discussion of women's ordination in the MB church received more prominence in the 1960s, it had already begun in the 1950s.

Prior to 1957, both married and single MB female missionaries were ordained for mission work; the ordination procedure was the same for both men and women. Between 1919 and 1956, thirty-seven women, nineteen of whom were single, were ordained in the MB Church in Canada.[7] It is not readily apparent why a suggestion was made at the General Conference level in 1954, "that the Conference consider whether it wouldn't be better that women missionaries be commissioned and not ordained."[8] After three years of study, the following resolution on the ordination of women was accepted, changing the former method of ordination to commissioning:

> In view of the fact that we as an MB Church, on the basis of clearly conceived scriptural convictions, do not admit sisters to the public gospel preaching ministry on par with brethren, we as a Conference designate the fact of setting aside sisters to missionary work "a commissioning" rather than "an ordination".[9]

The only grounds for the rescindment of women's ordination seemed to be "clearly conceived scriptural convictions."[10] Presented as part of a larger set of recommendations clarifying MB policies with regard to licensing and ordination, the context for the resolution on ordination was a general tightening of control in order to ensure responsible leadership. The resolution stated that

> it [licensing] authorizes a given person to preach the Gospel . . . but only within the confines of said Christian work project. Ordination to the gospel ministry should be extended exclusively to Christian workers who are acceptable for the ministry . . . and who are definitely and honestly desirous to labor within the said framework.[11]

While on the one hand Mennonite women were restricted in the institutional church, on the other hand, there were instances when women were encouraged and even commended in their role within women's societies. In 1966, John H. Redekop observed that at annual church conferences, MB women, who were not official delegates, were relegated to rear pews while their husbands, who were delegates, were ushered to front row seats.[12] Redekop was concerned that an outsider to the Mennonite tradition "might well conclude that our whole denomination is one great big men's fellowship."[13] The solution, Redekop suggested, was to affirm women in "women's work," i.e., the work of Ladies' Aid groups, a work which he felt should be "fully recognized as a regular branch of the church."[14] In the same year, the annual conference of the Ontario Conference of MB Churches made a public statement about the work of women's societies, commending them for their "many hours of labor and sacrificial giving in support of our institutions and the missions program."[15] On another occasion, a male speaker at the 1964 B.C. annual MB women's meeting referred to women's society work as "their rightful place in Christian service."[16] Thus, Mennonite women were encouraged to continue their work as participants in women's societies. This was considered to be their appropriate place of service in the church.

Concurrent with the church's encouragement that women continue their work through women's societies was an elevation of their role as homemakers and mothers, which was also supported by references to biblical texts. The role of Mennonite women as mothers and homemakers was discussed frequently in church periodicals during this time period. In 1954, a two-part article in a CMC paper, written by a male minister, underlines the extent to which this belief was based upon biblical teaching. The first article, "The husband's part in happy home building," based on Eph. 5:22 and 1 Cor. 11:3, emphasized the husband's role as "head" both in the home and in the church: "As men we are to assume the final leadership in the home and the church because God has endowed us with qualities of leadership and strength for such tasks."[17] As head of the wife, the husband was seen as the senior partner in the marriage; "in case of a tie, we [husbands] may cast the deciding vote."[18] The second article in the series, "The wife's part in happy home building," was also based on biblical texts.[19] Referring to Eph. 5:23 and 1 Pet. 3:1,2, the author stressed the importance of subjection of wives to husbands: "When a wife will not live in subjection to her head, she is disobeying God and will suffer consequences."[20] Based on Tit. 2:4-5 and Proverbs 31, he concluded that if a wife failed in her responsibility of making the home a cheerful, clean place, "she is out of the will of God."[21] In addition, the author claimed that according to 1 Tim. 5:14 and Ps. 127:3, it was women's "ordained responsibility to bear children willingly and rear them in the fear of the Lord."[22] That care of children was specifically women's work, and a degrading thing for men to do, is illustrated in a story of a new immigrant to Canada, who

> did not so much mind the farm work on the yard and on the fields, but when he was assigned to the dark *Sommerstube* (summer room) to sit between two cradles and rock the twins, while his employers slept, his warm blood turned warmer; if he was destined to make his living babysitting in this new country, he would soon return to where he came from.[23]

Similarly, within the MB tradition, the husband was considered head of the wife and the wife submissive to her husband's authority: "The wife must remember that leadership also means authority . . . someone must cast the deciding vote. This responsibility God has given to the husband."[24] Besides the injunctions in church periodicals, Mennonite women heard similar themes in sermons. One such address, given to MB women's societies in 1957, emphasized that "although women will always continue to be subordinate to men in the actual work of teaching, and directing in the church, they are the ones who will through the home provide the main motivation for missions in their influence upon others."[25]

While a survey of church periodical literature gives us an indication of the perception of women's role from the perspective of Mennonite male writers, we need to ask what women themselves believed their role to be. Were they satisfied with their subordinate role?

Based on the words and writings of Mennonite women during this time period, it appears that the role suggested by male church leaders was generally accepted by Mennonite women. In the 1968 Canadian Women's Conference of the CMC, the importance of women's place in the home was affirmed as their "most effective field of service. . . . Our Christian witness can be reflected through the lives of our children and influence of our husband. We feel a need to commit ourselves anew to the faithful service of dedicated builders of the home."[26] Several articles in the *Canadian Mennonite* elevated the career of homemaking, indicating its complexities, value, and fulfilment.[27] In 1956 and 1957, Anne Bargen used her regular column, "Conversation with mothers," to discuss various aspects of woman's role as wife and mother. In one of the articles, "Too gifted to become a mere housewife?" Bargen challenged her readers to contemplate the fact that it had been because of their mothers that great men of the past had been able to make significant contributions.[28] "Making a marriage last," another article in this series, gives an indication of the extent to which women themselves believed they should be subject to their husbands and aim to please them. The writer suggested that "if your husband wishes you different, why not change now?"[29] The "Prayer of a Young Wife" shows the lengths to which women believed they should go in order to serve their husbands:

> Oh may he (husband) never find
> That I am less than what he thinks!
> Lord, help me to be kind.
> I must have faith to meet his doubt,
> And strength, when he is weak.
>
> . . . .
>
> Lord help me always to maintain
> The standards of his creed,
> And give me courage, strength and love,
> To answer constant need.[30]

In the 1960s, other regular columns designed to appeal to homemakers appeared in church periodicals. In the CMC church periodical, Hedy Durksen's column, "Just around the house," continued from 1961 to 1962.[31] Then from 1965 to 1970, Anna L. Schroeder was responsible for the column, "In and out of my window."[32] The MB Church periodical also carried a regular column for women called, "Homemakers." A 1964 article in this serial affirmed that woman "was created for the help and happiness of man and for the glory of God" and that "motherhood is the highest calling to which a woman can attain."[33] While Mennonite women generally accepted their role as mothers and homemakers, some had begun to question it (as discussed in chapter 7).

Just as women accepted their role in the home, they also accepted their place in the church. They assumed male interpretations of biblical texts to be true; they did not question their invisibility in church leadership. Instead, they emphasized other opportunities of service and looked for different ways to make their contribution. In a three part series entitled, "The Ministry of Women in the Christian Church," an MB woman suggested that prayer, hospitality, missions, music and literature were important areas for women's involvement in the church.[34] Manitoba women of the CMC affirmed that although women's role appeared at times to be insignificant, "work behind the scenes is often the most important."[35] On another occasion, Hedy Durksen advocated that churches organize separate Sunday school classes for women, a method which had been successful in the church she attended. This, she felt, would enable women to participate more freely:

> Whereas before we ladies could sit quietly by and let the menfolk do all
> the talking, we now find that the discussion in class depends on us . . .
> granted, that our thoughts and expressions are not as profound and deep
> as those of our men, but I dare to think that we are perhaps more
> practical and down-to-earth in our approach.[36]

The value of a separate class for women, according to Durksen, was that women were able to share their ideas openly, something she said had been lacking in Mennonite churches.[37]

Durksen's suggestion of a separate class for Mennonite women gives us a clue as to why Mennonite women's societies flourished during this period. At a time when Mennonite women were restricted in church roles, here was a forum in which they could express themselves freely. Just like Sunday school classes for women only, the Mennonite women's society was a context in which Mennonite women could offer their opinions, make their own decisions, and assume leadership roles. It gave them an outlet for service at a time when homemaking, motherhood, and subordination in church and home were not only encouraged but biblically defended.

At the same time as the church restricted women's roles, they sought to establish greater links with women's societies; this was not unique to the Mennonites. In 1960, the Board of World Mission of the Presbyterian Church decided to assume the function of sending out missionaries, a job which until then had been the responsibility of the Women's Missionary Society.[38] In 1962, the United Church of Canada decided to amalgamate the Women's Association and the Women's Missionary Society into one group called United Church Women (UCW).[39] While this union was designed to make women's work more efficient, the Women's Missionary Society lost its administrative and financial autonomy.[40] Now funds were channelled through the finance committees of each congregation. Some women felt that "the larger institution (the church) was swallowing the smaller (the woman's organizations) in a process of cooptation . . . many WA and WMS women still felt no ownership of the new organization. It was, in their view, something imposed on them by 'head office' ".[41] Whether intentionally or not, in both the Presbyterian and the United Church the new arrangements meant that the church had greater control of women's groups.

The phenomenon of closer linkages, and thus, control of women's societies by the institutional church was also a reality in the Mennonite community. Official links with the church were formed when the church included Mennonite women's societies in church constitutions, and when it requested that women's societies give official reports of their activities at annual provincial and

national church conferences.[42]   In 1961, "the Board of Missions of the
Conference of Mennonites in Canada had made the request that a report on the
activities of the women's mission societies be read at the general session of the
conference during the period allotted to the Mission Board, and so this was
done."[43]   Unlike the discomfort the United Church women felt with the
intervention of the institutional church, Mennonite women seemed to welcome
these closer links and did not view it as negative control. Women's societies of
the Conference of MB Churches of Ontario were "thankful that an article
concerning the Women's Missionary Service has been added to the constitution
[of the Conference of the MB Churches of Ontario]. We are a part of the
conference structure [Conference of the MB Churches of Ontario]. We
appreciate this."[44] Since Mennonite women's societies considered themselves to
be a vital part of the church's program, they were happy to support the church's
projects through conference structures of the institutional church. Societies in
the Mennonite Conference of Alberta and the Conference of MB Churches of
Ontario serve as examples:

> . . . as an auxiliary of the Mennonite Conference of Alberta, we have
> supported the Conference projects to the best of our ability.[45]
>
> To serve the Lord heartily and willingly has been the concern of the
> Women's Missionary Service of the Ontario Mennonite Brethren
> Church. It is also our concern that we do this primarily through our
> Conference [Conference of the MB Churches of Ontario].[46]

For Mennonite women, closer links with the church meant a recognition by the
church that the work of Mennonite women's societies was indeed an valued
contribution. It put an official stamp of approval on their efforts. It meant that,
although women were restricted in their roles in the church, their contribution
through their societies was appreciated by the larger church. Church women's
societies was one context in which they could freely exercise their gifts and
contribute in their own way to the mission of the church.

Notes

1   Prentice et al., *Canadian Women*, p. 316.
2   Davy, *Women, Work and Worship*, p. 55.
3   Larry Kehler. "The secretary," *The Canadian Mennonite* 10 (23 March 1962): 2.
4   I. W. Redekopp, "The Woman's Place in the Church," *Mennonite Brethren Herald* 2, 11
    (15 March 1963): 5.
5   Ibid.
6   David Ewert, "Women in the Church," *Mennonite Brethren Herald* 5, 8 (25 February
    1966): 6.
7   Board of Foreign Missions, *Missionary Album* (Hillsboro: Conference of the Mennonite
    Brethren Church, 1956).
8   *Yearbook of the Forty-Sixth General Conference of the Mennonite Brethren Church of
    North America* (Hillsboro: Mennonite Brethren Publishing House, 1954), p. 6.
9   Ibid., p. 106.
10 Specific biblical texts were not mentioned in the recommendation.

11 *Yearbook of the Forty-Seventh General Conference of the Mennonite Brethren Church of North America* (Hillsboro: Mennonite Brethren Publishing House, 1957), p. 106.

12 John H. Redekop, "Women–Second Class Christians," *Mennonite Brethren Herald* 5, 23 (24 June 1966): 2.

13 Ibid.

14 Ibid.

15 Edward Boldt, ed., *A History of the Ontario Conference of Mennonite Brethren Churches: 1957-1982* (N.p., 1982), p. 37.

16 Mrs. Ernest Dyck, "BC Missionary Fellowship annual meeting," *Mennonite Brethren Herald* 3, 42 (23 October 1964): 17.

17 B. Charles Hostetter, "The husband's part in happy home building," *The Canadian Mennonite* 2 (27 August 1954): 6.

18 Ibid.

19 B. Charles Hostetter, "The wife's part in happy home building," *The Canadian Mennonite* 2 (3 September 1954): 6.

20 Ibid.

21 Ibid.

22 Ibid.

23 "Portrait of a Pioneer. Heinrich H. Hamm pioneered in civic and church affairs," *The Canadian Mennonite* 2 (20 August 1954): 4.

24 Jacob Suderman, "Christian Authority for Marriage and the Home," *Mennonite Brethren Herald* 1, 36 (28 September 1962): 6,7. Eph. 5:22; 6:4; and 1 Cor. 11:3 are used to defend husbands' authority.

25 "The place of women in church work today," *The Canadian Mennonite* 5 (18 October 1957): 1.

26 Mrs. Henry Funk, "Women stress foreign missions and the home," *The Canadian Mennonite* 16 (13 August 1968): 14.

27 Helen Dick, "A mother and her career child," *The Canadian Mennonite* 17 (26 September 1969): 11; "What's a good wife worth?" *The Canadian Mennonite* 13 (28 September 1965): 12; and Hedy Durksen, "Is life passing you by?" *The Canadian Mennonite* 9 (3 February 1961): 1.

28 Anne Bargen, "Too gifted to become a mere housewife?" *The Canadian Mennonite* 4 (7 September 1956): 2. Bargen refers to mothers of Moses, Wesley, Moody, and Lincoln.

29 Anne Bargen, "Making a marriage last," *The Canadian Mennonite* 4 (28 September 1956): 4.

30 Ibid.

31 "A new feature begins in this issue," *The Canadian Mennonite* 9 (3 February 1961): 1.

32 Anna L. Schroeder, "In and out of my window," *The Canadian Mennonite* 13 (7 September 1965): 12.

33 Hilda Froese, "The Ministry of Women in the Christian Church," Part 1, *Mennonite Brethren Herald* 3 ,21 (22 May 1964): 13. Reference is made to Eve and Rebecca as women who were a bad influence; Ruth, Mary, and Eunice as women who were good mothers.

34 Hilda Froese, "The Ministry of Women in the Christian Church," Parts 1-3, *Mennonite Brethren Herald* 3, 21 (22 May 1964): 13; 25 (19 June 1964): 13; 27 (3 July 1964): 12. Reference is made to Hannah (1 Sam. 1:27), the Shunamite woman, Lydia (Acts 16:15), Priscilla (Rom. 16:3) and to the woman of Prov. 31:20.

35 Elsie Neufeld, "Manitoba women met at Boissevain," *The Canadian Mennonite* 11 (7 June 1963): 3.

36 Hedy Durksen, "The ladies' class," *The Canadian Mennonite* 9 (23 June 1961): 7.

37 Ibid.

38 Interview with Joan Sampson, 1988.
39 Davy, *Women, Work and Worship*, p. 53.
40 Ibid., p. 52.
41 Ibid., p. 54.
42 Hooge, *The History of the Canadian Women in Mission*, p. 19, and Boldt, ed. *A History of the Ontario Conference of Mennonite Brethren Churches*, p. 36.
43 Hooge, *The History of the Canadian Women in Mission*, p. 19
44 Olga G. Enns, "Women's Missionary Service," in *Yearbook of the Thirty-Fifth Annual Provincial Conference of the Mennonite Brethren Churches in Ontario* (N.p.: Conference of the Mennonite Brethren Churches of Ontario, 1966), p. 90.
45 Neufeld, ed., *History of Alberta Mennonite Women in Mission*, p. 9.
46 Olga G. Enns, "Women's Missionary Service," p. 90.

6

The Flowering

Canadian Mennonite women's societies were not unique in their experience of numerical growth in the 1950s and 1960s. Other women's organizations, both secular and religious, were flourishing as well. During this time, Women's Institutes in Canada expanded their activities as they tried to improve the quality of life for Canadian women. Church women's groups were also thriving; membership in United Church women's groups reached an all time high in 1962.[1] In the Mennonite community, participation in women's societies was also on the rise. Unlike today, most Mennonite women who were members of a Mennonite church were also members of a Mennonite women's society. As younger women joined already existent societies, groups became too large and the age difference among members was too great. For these reasons, a practice developed such that additional groups were formed for younger women; as the Busy Fingers Sewing Circle of the Bergthal Mennonite Church in Didsbury expressed it, "the reasons for organizing another aid were several. Young married women with similar interests wanted to get together for fellowship. The existing group was quite large, and some women did not want to belong to the same group as their mothers."[2] Depending on the size of the local congregation, there were from one to six separate women's groups in each local church.

Table 4 includes the number of CMC and MB Mennonite women's societies between 1953 and 1988 among churches formed between 1874 and 1952.[3]

Table 4
Increase in Mennonite Women's Societies

Time Period	Increase in CMC Women's Societies	Increase in MB Women's Societies	Total Increase
1953-1959	46	17	63
1960-1969	23	16	39
1970-1979	9	6	15
1980-1987	4	7	11

The greatest number of additional societies were formed in the seven years from 1953 to 1959. In the seventeen year period between 1953 and 1969, 102 new groups were organized, whereas in the next eighteen year period, only twenty-six were formed.

Women's societies grew not only in number, but also in their tendency to form their own organizational structures. In the CMC, they had already organized themselves provincially in British Columbia, Alberta, Saskatchewan, Manitoba, and Ontario in the 1930s and 1940s,[4] and in 1952, established a national organization, namely, CWM.[5] Women in the MB tradition, however, were not organized provincially until the 1950s. The first to do so were MB women's societies in British Columbia who formed the MB Church Ladies Aid of British Columbia in 1953/1954.[6] In Saskatchewan, because there were two district church conferences (one in the north and one in the south), two women's conferences were formed: Women's Missionary Fellowship in the north, organized in 1958, and Women's MB Missionary Auxiliary in the south in 1959.[7] In 1960 and 1967 respectively, Ontario and Manitoba MB women established provincial organizations.[8] No formal provincial body was ever formed in Alberta, although women's groups within the province have met for annual gatherings.[9]

Women established provincial and national organizations so that they could work more systematically and more effectively for the cause of missions. The goal of the Manitoba MB women's organization was "to unite their efforts more effectively and to be able to promote the cause of missions more effectively."[10] When MB women's societies formed a provincial organization in British Columbia, their plan was to "unite as a provincial group to augment the activities of the many women's groups in the local churches."[11] In southern Saskatchewan, MB women stated that they hoped "to work more efficiently in the interest of missions."[12] Women in Ontario viewed their organization as "a means of co-ordinating activities among ladies' groups and initiating projects in which all could participate."[13] Provincial and national structures were regarded as vehicles through which women's societies' work for missions could be enhanced.

As new Mennonite women's societies were organized, women gave them names. In the years of establishment, Mennonite women's societies most frequently called themselves missions, sewing, aid, or service group; they knit and sewed to support missions projects. Naming was an expression of their identity. Between 1953 and 1969, some shifts in naming began to occur. First, some of those groups which were already in existence changed their names. Among these, the most notable change was to names denoting fellowship, such as from "Busy Bees Circle" to "Women's Fellowship" and from "*Nähverein*" to "Ladies Fellowship." Second, as younger women started their own groups, the names given to these new societies also showed a shift in group identity. (See tables 5 and 6.)

Names denoting missions and aid/help/service still predominated, however, there were two major shifts during this time period. The first was a decrease in the number of groups that called themselves sewing societies.

Table 5
Percentage Distribution of Names of CMC Women's Societies
1953-1969

CATEGORY	NAMES	NUMBER	PERCENTAGE
Missions	Sunshine Mission Circle, Loving Deeds Mission Circle, Women's Missionary Society, Mission Helpers (2x), Goodwill Mission Circle, Women in Mission, Mission Circle, Ladies Mission Group, Missionettes, *Missionsverein*	11	16
Sewing	Sunbeam Sewing Circle, Junior Sewing Circle, Busy Fingers Sewing Circle, *Nähverein*	4	6
Aid/Help/Service	Young Women's Charity Club, Willing Hands Ladies Aid, Women's Christian Endeavour, Servettes, Willing Workers, Helping Hands (4x), Willing Hands, Goodwill Society, Goodwill Club, Good Samaritan Club, Willing Helpers (2x), Goodwill Workers, *Wohltätigkeitsverein*, Women's Auxiliary, Ladies Aid (6x)	24	35
Biblical Woman's Name & Aid	Magdalene Ladies Aid	1	1
Biblical Woman's Name	Tabitha Circle, Maria Martha Women's Society, *Tabea Verein*	3	4
Fellowship	Harmony Hearts, Homemakers Fellowship (3x), Fellowship Group, Friendship Circle, Women's Christian Fellowship, Ladies Fellowship, *Koinonia* Ladies Group, Women's Fellowship, Christian Fellowship	11	16
Other	Young Women's, Guiding Mothers, Morija Circle, Homemakers, *Verein* (11x)	15	22[14]
TOTAL		69	100

While 17 percent of CMC societies and 25 percent of MB societies were called sewing societies between 1874 and 1952 (see tables 2 and 3 in Chapter 4) now only 6 percent of CMC and 3 percent of MB societies were designated in this way. This shift represented a change in focus for women's societies which is corroborated in an article about the first one hundred years of the MB church (1860-1960). The writer acknowledges in the article that "there has been a change in recent years. The shift of emphasis has been from sewing circles to mission circles. Greater emphasis is being placed on study, devotions and programs of activity which shall not supplant but be complementary to the working with hands."[15] This shift in emphasis from sewing to missions is reflected in the naming of Mennonite women's societies; the percentage of names referring to sewing decreased substantially and the number of names exemplifying a focus on missions, aid, help, or service remained almost the same.

The second major change was a shift to names denoting fellowship. We have already noted that among societies who changed their names during this time, the most significant change was to names designating fellowship.

Table 6
Percentage Distribution of Names of MB Women's Societies
1953-1969

CATEGORY	NAMES	NUMBER	PERCENTAGE
Missions	Junior Ladies Missionary Prayer Group, Ladies Missionary Prayer Group, Missionary Prayer Group, Sunbeam Mission Band, The Mission Group, Ladies Mission Circle, Mission *Verein*	7	21
Sewing	Ladies Sewing Circle	1	3
Aid/Help/Service	Women's Ministries, Willing Helpers (3x), Good Samaritan Club, Christian Service Club, Work and Prayer Group, *Frauendienst*, Ladies Aid, Auxiliary	10	31
Missions & Fellowship	Missionary Fellowship Group	1	3
Biblical Woman's Name	Dorcas Ladies Group (2x), Mary Martha Group, Mary Martha *Verein*	4	12
Fellowship	Ladies Fellowship (2x), Christian Fellowship, Christian Fellowship Guild, Ladies Christian Fellowship Group, *Schwesternbund*	6	18
Other	Pleasant Hour, Sunshine Club, Marantha, *Verein*	4	12
TOTAL		33	100

Similarly, among newly established women's societies, there was also an increase in names denoting fellowship. Among CMC groups, fellowship groups comprised only 2.5 percent of names between 1874 and 1952, but 16 percent between 1953 and 1969. Among MB groups, 15 percent were called fellowship groups between 1874 and 1952, and 21 percent between 1953 and 1969. However, despite the trend toward names of fellowship, a missions/service emphasis still remained predominant between 1953 and 1969, with 58 percent of CMC and MB women's societies functioning under the rubric of mission, sewing, aid, helping, or service. (See tables 5 and 6.)

With provincial and national women's organizations in place and with the increase in the number of women's societies, it is not surprising that the years between 1953 and 1969 was a time when Mennonite women lived to the full the paradigm they had established in the first half of the twentieth century. This meant an even stronger commitment to their goals of missions and fellowship. Newly organized societies often explicitly stated their purpose at the point of their establishment. The following two serve as examples:

> On February 22, 1960, a small group of sisters felt led of the Lord to gather for fellowship and prayer. . . . The purpose of the Mission Group is not only to fellowship but also to further the interest in missions.[16]

> The Arnaud Christian Fellowship was organized on November 27, 1962. . . . The purpose of the group was to help with mission projects at home and abroad, to promote and encourage interest in missions and to further our own Christian growth.[17]

Constitutions, such as that of the Goodwill Club in Coaldale Mennonite Church, also reflected this emphasis. Their constitution specified three group objectives:

1. To have Christian fellowship with other women.
2. To have group discussions, including Bible studies, and guest speakers.
3. Through an organized group to become an integral part of the work of the church:
   a. in the church structure - participating in church activities
   b. in the community - i.e., hospital visitation
   c. in foreign mission fields.[18]

In 1953, one year after the organization of Canadian Women in Mission (CWM), this national group accepted a constitution that outlined two purposes for the organization: "(a) To encourage a personal dedication of each member to Christ and His work, and (b) To support and promote missions and other conference causes in our churches."[19] The 1964 Constitution of the Women's MB Missionary Auxiliary of South Saskatchewan also stated its purpose:

1. To promote unified spiritual fellowship with all the individual groups participating.
2. To engage in practical work, working toward unified projects for our MB mission fields. These projects are:
   a. outfitting missionaries going to the foreign field from our district
   b. new projects as agreed upon at our meetings.[20]

At the first Manitoba MB women's conference women decided that "mission effort and enterprise . . . should continue to receive major emphasis."[21] In Ontario as well, the focus was missions. A 1966 provincial conference of the Ontario Women's Missionary Service stated that their goal was "to serve the Lord heartily and willingly."[22] Thus, constitutions show the strong emphasis on both missions and "Christian" or "spiritual" fellowship.

The overwhelming majority of Mennonite women's societies at local, provincial, and national levels gave practical expression to their commitment to missions by their impressive support of many service-oriented projects between 1953 and 1969.[23] Women's groups often responded to several needs at a time,[24] including foreign mission projects, home mission projects,[25] MCC, denominational schools, community needs, and local church needs. The 1961 financial statement of the Friendly Hour Club of First Mennonite Church in Saskatoon, for example, reported the following distribution of funds:

> $65.00 for two radio programs
> $100.00 for missions
> $15.00 for Rosthern Junior College
> $20.00 for Winnipeg Bible College
> $10.00 for the Seminary
> $10.00 for the British and Foreign Bible Society
> $15.00 for the general fund in First Mennonite Church
> $15.00 for the building fund at First Mennonite Church.[26]

Women in this society designated a considerable amount of money for missions. The $100.00 given for missions represents 40 percent of the total amount. Similarly, at the provincial level, a large proportion of funds was collected for mission projects. In 1961, the two thousand dollar budget of the South Saskatchewan MB Ladies Auxiliary went entirely for mission projects; two-thirds of it was earmarked for foreign missions (including mission work in Japan, Peru, and Columbia) and one-third for home missions (including salaries of Saskatchewan MB missionaries).[27] At a national level the CWM of the CMC designated all of its funds to service oriented projects in 1967 as follows:

Total Income	**$185,324.61**
Total Disbursement	**168,952.48**
Foreign Missions	33,320.94
Home Missions	21,382.51
Local Needs	27,122.57
Schools: Bible, High, College, etc.	6,768.41
Relief–Cash	10,756.16
Cash for Christmas Bundles	11,733.35

(not to mention the pounds of bandages rolled, blankets and layettes sewn, soap donated, et cetera.) [28]

In this case, 32 percent of disbursements were for foreign and home missions. The remainder was used for other service needs.

While women continued to support missions/service projects in the 1950s and 1960s, their methods of fundraising underwent substantial changes. Survey responses and women's own society reports point to significant changes from raising money through auctions, bake sales, bazaars, and catering through fundraising by cash donations or offerings. The Bergthal Sewing Circle of the Bergthal Mennonite Church in Didsbury, for example, having begun mission sales soon after the organization of their group in 1929, referred to a change in fundraising in the late 1960s. They reported that "as times changed, so did our methods of operation. 1968 saw our last Mission Sale, and we now use the 'donation' system to raise money."[29]   Clearly, methods of fundraising had changed; but what lay behind the shift?

There were two primary reasons why fundraising methods began to change. The first had to do with the perceived appropriateness of the auction as a fundraising method. There developed in the late 1940s a sense that the auction sale was not a proper way for church groups to raise money for missions. This trend among Mennonite women's societies, originating in the General Conference Women's Missionary Association (WMA) Executive of North America,[30] resulted in a cessation of this method in the United States by 1947.[31] Thereafter, Marie Lohrentz, WMA president of North America, also came to Canada to try to convince CMC women that auctions were not appropriate ways to raise money.[32] Lohrentz was not entirely successful at first, but eventually, auctions became a less popular mode of fundraising among CMC women's societies as well.   The same phenomenon occurred among MB women's societies, i e , a decline in using the auction as a method of raising money for missions.[33]

A second reason for the change in fundraising is that women did not seem to have time to keep up with quilting and baking. A poem written by one local Mennonite women's society expresses this well:

After seven long years of having aid
A constitution was finally made . . .
A group like this you'll rarely see
With 25 kids and mom's 23
On May the 4th in sixty-six
Laverne's birthday party, what a fix!
All those kids–Oh what a crowd
He was six and he was proud. . . .
In February '67 we'd just had enough
Of ordering remnants and sewing stuff
To make clothes for children and also for us
It wasn't worth the bother–just too much fuss. [34]

Women were simply too busy with their own families and did not seem to have as much time to knit and sew for mission projects.

As in the past, the commitment of Mennonite women's societies to the support of missions remained firmly based on biblical texts which they chose as group mottos and themes for conferences and retreats. It was customary for a women's society to choose a biblical text as a motto at the point of the establishment of the group. The Women's Auxiliary of the First Mennonite Church in Saskatoon tells the story of their beginning: "Nineteen years ago the Women's Auxiliary came into being. It was founded on January 13, 1958, with 16 ladies in attendance who preferred English at the meetings. . . . We adopted as our motto: 'Serve him with a perfect heart and willing mind.' I Chr. 28:9."[35] Biblical texts which CMC and MB Mennonite women's societies chose as mottos during these years include the following:

>By love serve one another. (Gal. 5:13)
>
>She stretcheth out her hand to the poor; yea, she reacheth forth her hands to the needy. (Pro. 31:20)
>
>But to do good and to communicate forget not: for with such sacrifices God is well pleased. (Heb. 13:16)
>
>For we are labourers together with God: ye are God's husbandry,[36] ye are God's building. (1 Cor. 3:9) (Motto of three groups)
>
>And whatsoever ye do, do it heartily, as to the Lord and not unto men. (Col. 3:23) (Motto of two groups)
>
>Go ye therefore and teach all nations, baptizing them in the name of the Father and of the Son and of the Holy Ghost: teaching them to observe all things whatsoever I have commanded you: and, lo, I am with you always, even unto the end of the world. (Matt. 28:19,20)
>
>Looking unto Jesus the author and finisher of our faith; who for the joy that was set before him endured the cross, despising the shame, and is set down at the right hand of the throne of God. (Heb. 12:2)
>
>Serve him with a perfect heart and willing mind. (1 Chr. 28:9)
>
>And whatsoever ye do in word or deed, do all in the name of the Lord Jesus, giving thanks to God and the Father by him. (Col. 3:17)
>
>And let us not be weary in well doing: for in due season we shall reap, if we faint not. As we have therefore opportunity, let us do good unto all men, especially unto them who are of the household of faith. (Gal. 6:9, 10) (Gal. 6:9 chosen by two groups; Gal. 6:10 chosen by one group; and Gal. 6:9, 10 chosen by one group)
>
>For the love of Christ constraineth us; because we thus judge, that if one died for all, then were all dead: Now then we are ambassadors for Christ, as though God did beseech you by us: we pray you in Christ's stead, be ye reconciled to God. (2 Cor. 5:15, 20)
>
>Therefore, my beloved brethren, be ye steadfast, unmoveable, always abounding in the work of the Lord, forasmuch as ye know that your labour is not in vain in the Lord. (1 Cor. 15:58) (Motto chosen by two groups)
>
>Let your light so shine before men, that they may see your good works, and glorify your Father which is in heaven. (Matt. 5:16)
>
>Serve the Lord with gladness: come before his presence with singing. (Ps. 100:2)
>
>. . . And who is my neighbour? . . . Which now of these three, thinkest thou, was neighbour unto him that fell among the thieves? And he said, He that shewed mercy on him. Then said Jesus unto him, Go, and do thou likewise. (Lk. 10:28-37)
>
>Whatever therefore ye eat, or drink, or whatsoever ye do, do all to the glory of God. (1 Cor. 10:31)
>
>But seek ye first the kingdom of God, and his righteousness; and all these things shall be added unto you. (Matt. 6:33)

Most of these biblical references emphasize service, as indicated by the use of words and phrases such as "serve," "stretcheth out her hand," "reacheth forth her hands to the needy," "do good," "labourers," "serve him," "word or deed," "well doing," "work of the Lord," "your labour," "good works," and "do thou likewise." According to Mennonite women, their service had a biblical basis; the work of their societies was inspired by a biblical faith.

In addition to biblical mottos, Mennonite women also chose biblical texts for themes at retreats and conferences of Mennonite women's societies. Between 1953 and 1969, themes for CMC and MB provincial and national women's conferences included "Women's Service for God" (Lk. 10:38-42); "Motive and Objective of Missions" (1 Cor. 3:9; 2 Cor. 5:14); "Give Ye Them to Eat" (Lk. 9:13); and "Who is My Neighbor?" (1 Pet. 2:17a).[37] That Mennonite women chose biblical texts to motivate them to service shows that they felt their mandate came from the Bible. They felt responsible to obey it and believed that their service efforts were in fact an expression of obedience to the word of God, as they understood it. The texts chosen for mottos and biblical themes for conferences were consistent with their identity expressed in naming and with their actions to support the missions effort.

While the focus of Mennonite women's societies in these years continued to have a strong service element, women still participated in regular meetings which had a strong spiritual focus. As one group recounts, the format for the worship ritual remained essentially the same as before:

> The meetings were opened by the president with scripture reading, prayer and singing. During the meeting one member would read aloud from an inspirational book while the rest knitted and sewed for the Red Cross and for MCC. A collection was taken at every meeting and a lunch served.[38]

As in the past, Mennonite women's societies continued to be contexts of spiritual strengthening. That Mennonite women considered their worship to be biblically based is illustrated in a discussion in a church periodical in 1966, in which the writer, a member of a Mennonite women's society, referred to first century worship in Corinth. While on the one hand, she felt that Mennonite church services were not sufficiently styled on the New Testament pattern, on the other hand, she suggested that a New Testament worship style would be more likely to happen in the context of women's society meetings than within the larger church context.[39] The fact that she would even compare women's society meetings to New Testament patterns of worship indicates that she felt women's societies were forums for regular worship. This gives further confirmation to the idea that Mennonite women's societies functioned as a parallel church for Mennonite women. As Katie Funk Wiebe states,

> these women's groups were transplanted to America from Russia and here underwent various transformations, sometimes functioning as an auxiliary to the church and later on sometimes almost as a church in themselves, operating almost parallel to the congregation with its own

budget, aggressive program, membership list, and annual meetings and retreats.[40]

Mennonite women's societies became a context where Mennonite women could be full participants in every aspect of worship and, at the same time, become involved in missions and service in their own way.

Notes

1 Gillian Sniatynski, "UCW at 25: Marys or Marthas?" *The Observer* (1987): 30.
2 Neufeld, ed., *History of Alberta Mennonite Women in Mission*, p. 72.
3 Obtained from information in Bartel, *Saskatchewan Women in Mission*; Neufeld, ed., *History of Alberta Mennonite Women in Mission*; Hildegard Fiss, *The Story of Women in Mission (Southwest Ontario)* (N.p., 1976); Froese, *Manitoba Mennonite Women in Mission*; Rempel, *History of B.C. Mennonite Women in Mission*; histories of CMC and MB local churches; and responses to the survey on CMC and MB women's societies.
4 Hooge, *The History of the Canadian Women in Mission*, pp. 4, 7, 10.
5 Ibid.
6 Wiebe, ed., *A Century of Grace and Witness*, pp. 74.
7 Ibid., pp. 73-74.
8 "Report of the Women's Conference of the Manitoba Mennonite Brethren Churches," Women's Conference of the Manitoba Mennonite Brethren Churches, 17 June 1967.
9 Interview with Heidi Kornelsen, Edmonton, Alberta, August 1987.
10 Mrs. W. Regehr, President, Women's Conference of the Manitoba Mennonite Brethren Churches, Letter to Board of Missions and Services, "Women's Conference of the Manitoba Mennonite Brethren Churches Minutes and Correspondence," 1967-1969.
11 Mrs. Ernest Dyck, "Women's meeting in BC," *Mennonite Brethren Herald* 3, 19 (8 May 1964): 13.
12 Minutes of the South Saskatchewan Mennonite Brethren Ladies Auxiliary, 1959-87.
13 Neoma Jantz, "Ontario ladies meet for spring rally," *Mennonite Brethren Herald* 3, 17 (24 April 24 1964): 13.
14 Wiebe, ed., *A Century of Grace and Witness (1860-1960)*, p. 74.
15 The percentage of the "Other" category is high because eleven women's societies called their groups simply, *Verein*.
16 *Mennonite Brethren Church Winkler, Manitoba (1888-1963)* (N.p., n.d.), p. 35.
17 Froese, *Manitoba Mennonite Women in Mission*, p. 21.
18 Neufeld, ed., *History of Alberta Mennonite Women in Mission*, p. 43.
19 "Constitution of Canadian Women in Mission," Canadian Women in Mission, 1953.
20 "Constitution of the Women's MB Missionary Auxiliary of South Saskatchewan," Women's Mennonite Brethren Missionary Auxiliary of South Saskatchewan, 1964.
21 "Women's Conference: MB Churches of Manitoba," in *1967 Yearbook of the Thirty-Third Annual Manitoba Conference of MB Churches* (Winnipeg: Conference of MB Churches of Manitoba, 1967), p. 111.
22 Enns, "Women's Missionary Service," p. 90.
23 Obtained from information in Bartel, *Saskatchewan Women in Mission*; Neufeld, ed., *History of Alberta Mennonite Women in Mission*; Fiss, *The Story of Women in Mission*; Froese, *Manitoba Mennonite Women in Mission*; Rempel, *History of B.C. Mennonite Women in Mission (1939-1976)*; histories of CMC and MB local churches; and responses to the survey on CMC and MB women's societies.

24 *"Die Arbeit des Frauenvereine der 'Ersten Mennonitengemeinde' in Winnipeg,"* (*Der Bote* (8 *Dezember* 1959): 1.

25 Home missions refers to mission programs in Canada, as opposed to foreign missions, which focused on mission programs overseas.

26 Annual report of Friendly Hour Club, First Mennonite Church, Saskatoon, Saskatchewan, 1961.

27 Minutes of the South Saskatchewan Mennonite Brethren Ladies Auxiliary, 1961.

28 Mrs. P. Redekopp, "Canadian Women's Missionary Conference–1967," *Yearbook: Conference of Mennonites in Canada,* (Winnipeg: Conference of Mennonites in Canada, 1967).

29 Neufeld, ed., *History of Alberta Mennonite Women in Mission,* p. 71.

30 This was the equivalent of the executive of CWM in Canada; members in both organizations belonged to the General Conference Mennonite Church of North America.

31 Goering, *Women in Search of Mission,* pp. 60-61.

32 Ibid.

33 Indicated by responses to the survey sent to CMC and MB women's societies in Canada.

34 Lillian Patkau et al., "Constitution," Magdalene Ladies Aid and Hanley Ladies Aid, 1982.

35 Bartel, *Saskatchewan Women in Mission,* p. 68.

36 Biblical references are from the King James Version, likely still the most commonly used Bible in Mennonite churches during this time period.

37 Minutes of the South Saskatchewan Mennonite Brethren Ladies Auxiliary; Rempel, *History of B.C. Mennonite Women in Mission,* pp. 20-21; and "Women's Conference Themes," Canadian Women in Mission.

38 Froese, *Manitoba Mennonite Women in Mission,* p. 30.

39 Lillian Giesbrecht, "What makes a ladies aid profitable?" *Mennonite Brethren Herald* 5, 22 (10 June 1966):16-17.

40 Katie Funk Wiebe, "Women in the Mennonite Brethren Church," in *Your Daughters Shall Prophesy: Women in Ministry in the Church,* ed., John E. Toews et al. (Winnipeg: Kindred Press, 1992), p. 183. This book was studied by MB congregations in preparation for their 1993 General Conference, when the issue of women's role in church ministry would be discussed.

7

Seeds of Questioning

While the dominant trend in the 1950s and 1960s was for Mennonite women to accept their role in the church, home, and women's society, the 1960s witnessed the seeds of questioning, seeds that would grow in the next two decades. Mennonite women wrote of the quandary in which they found themselves:

> The trouble seems to be that we women are no longer quite sure whether we belong in the home, whether we should be out getting more education so as to keep up with our well-educated husbands, or maybe have a career outside the home.
>
> Do we still teach our daughters that they are to be keepers of homes and the mothers of future generations, or is this being hopelessly old-fashioned? Just where do we go from here?[1]

This is not surprising, since women were getting mixed messages. Within society, women's choices in the areas of education and career were increasing because of the women's movement. At the same time, the church encouraged greater participation of women in the local congregation, yet they continued to advocate submission to husbands and male church leaders.

One specific point of contention was that of women's employment outside the home. The fact that an article in the 1950s argued that married Christian women should not be employed outside the home, indicates that this was probably beginning to happen in Mennonite circles.[2] Reference was made to women's "God-designated place and responsibilities . . . *Kirchen, Küchen* and *Kinder* (church, kitchen and children). And what a noble, biblical and satisfying calling this is! But it doesn't seem to satisfy the modern, trained, professing Christian woman."[3] Sometimes men and women disagreed on the advisability of becoming employed outside the home. The editor of *The Canadian Mennonite* felt women should be employed only in the case of financial need, "but this should never be considered a desirable arrangement. . . . raising children requires more imagination, creativity, patience, and any intellectual activity you can name, than almost any other occupation in the world."[4] Anna L. Schroeder found this attitude perplexing and suggested that women's employment might be a threat to males. She reassured men that "a great many women have no ambition to step outside their own homes, but just as many long to do something besides housework. Not just for the money they might earn, but for interest and enjoyment."[5]

While it was assumed that married women would be full time homemakers, single women could be employed outside the home with the church's blessing. An article on "The single girl" appeared in 1957 which emphasized the importance of the secretary to the Canadian businessman of "his 'girl Friday' who gives her undivided attention to his every beck and call."[6] A church vocation program was even initiated to assist single Mennonite women to find church-related jobs.[7]

Besides employment outside the home, some Mennonite women were interested in furthering their education; "some are sick of concerning themselves solely with marshmallow and jelly salads, and would prefer something which challenges their intellect."[8] Women's desire for personal development and intellectual growth led to an increase in the number of Mennonite women returning to school to pursue further studies.[9] Katie Funk Wiebe noted that the church was reluctant to condone this change because of its fear that women would neglect the home.[10]

At the same time as Mennonite women became interested in careers outside the home and educational advancement, some were beginning to question the role of women's societies. In 1963, a full page article in the Canadian Mennonite debated the effectiveness of the sewing circle.[11] Writer Katie Funk Wiebe referred to the sewing circle as a tradition that had enabled women "to use their skills as a homemaker in the service of the church," noting that in the past "they [women] have accepted thankfully and humbly the unique place of service" but now were questioning its place: "Does the traditional women's society invite the interest of the so-called 'intellectual'? Is the women's church organization of today really the vital arm of Christ it purports to be or merely a crutch under the arm of the men?"[12] The seeds of questioning had been sewn.

Even though some women were raising questions about the roles to which they had become accustomed, it is difficult to tell how widespread this new thinking was. The majority of Mennonite women seemed content to make their primary contribution to the church through the venue of women's societies. In 1969, the secretary-treasurer of the CMC Canadian Women's Missionary Conference defended women's groups as the best way for women to be involved in the church, and at the same time declared that women were not even aspiring to be ministers.[13] Some Mennonite women were at least aware of the issues of the women's movement as indicated in a book review of Betty Friedan's, *The Feminine Mystique* which appeared in *The Canadian Mennonite* in 1966. The writer admitted that suffragettes had gained certain privileges for women, even though, according to her, their methods and goals were not always right.[14] She agreed with Friedan that women were living below their capabilities and queried whether the Mennonite church had been guilty of asking too little of Mennonite women: "Too many women in our churches have yielded to an image which is less than biblical; their silence is empty and they have little to submit. . . . Is there a Mennonite feminine mystique?"[15] Implicit in the discussion was a critique of the way the Bible had been interpreted to keep Mennonite women submissive. This is a sign not only that women were beginning to question male-centered biblical interpretation and traditionally held positions in the church but also that Mennonite women were being influenced by society around them, in particular, the women's movement.

It is difficult to make causal links, however, it is noteworthy that during this era, increased involvement in women's societies coincided with both an increased affirmation of the importance of women's place in the home and emphasis on restrictions as to women's role in the church. If women could not serve God on church committees and as church leaders, they certainly could within the context of their societies. While this seemed to be the mentality of most Mennonite women who were members of Mennonite women's societies, a few lone voices, in both the CMC and MB Church, had begun to question the assumption that women should devote all their energies to homemaking and mothering. The following decades would witness continued discussion on the role of women and more widespread questioning of the place of women's societies.

Notes

1   Hedy Durksen, "Where do we stand?" *The Canadian Mennonite* 10 (30 March 1962): 8.
2   "Why Christian married women work," *The Canadian Mennonite* 3 (21 January 1955): 7.
3   Ibid.
4   Larry Kehler, "Mere motherhood?" *The Canadian Mennonite* 9 (4 August 1961): 2.
5   Anna L. Schroeder, "My husband won't let me," *The Canadian Mennonite* 14 (12 July 1966): 20.
6   "The single girl," *The Canadian Mennonite* 5 (4 October 1957): 2.
7   "Newton pioneers work program for women," *The Canadian Mennonite* 5 (25 January 1957): 1; and "Women in Church Vocations–A service and fellowship opportunity for girls," *The Canadian Mennonite* 6 (1 August 1958): 5. The program, entitled Women in Church Vocations, was initiated in 1957 by the General Conference Board of Christian Service (a board of the North American General Conference Church). Its aims were to recruit, train and place interested single women.
8   Katie Funk Wiebe, "The Women's Class," *Mennonite Brethren Herald* 6, 1 (6 January 1967): 16.
9   Katie Funk Wiebe, "Unfinished Business," *Mennonite Brethren Herald* 8, 26 (26 December 1969):18-19.
10 Ibid.
11 Katie Funk Wiebe, "The place of women in the work of the church," *The Canadian Mennonite* 11 (1 March 1963): 5.
12 Ibid.
13 Elaine Penner, "Few church women aspire to 'male' jobs–at least not yet," *The Canadian Mennonite* 17 (9 May 1969): 5.
14 Katie Funk Wiebe, "The feminine mystique (1)," *The Canadian Mennonite* 14 (29 March 1966): 52.
15 Katie Funk Wiebe, "The feminine mystique (2)," *The Canadian Mennonite* 14 (5 April 1966): 10.

PART FOUR

Change and Decline: 1970 -1995

8

Ambivalence about Women's Roles

The 1970s and 1980s was a time of significant change for women within Canadian society generally and within the Christian community in particular. The 1970 Royal Commission on the Status of Women brought a number of women's issues to the fore, among them that "women should be free to choose whether or not to take employment outside their homes," and that "the care of children is a responsibility to be shared by the mother, the father, and society."[1] In the church, by the late 1970s, women were admitted to ordination in several Protestant denominations, and women's issues raised in secular society were beginning to penetrate the Christian community. The Mennonite community did not remain unaffected by the women's movement.

While most CMC and MB Mennonite churches no longer adhered to the practice of *Bruderschaft*, men continued to hold the primary positions of leadership. In 1975, a Canadian MB conference resolution enabled women to serve as delegates to the Canadian MB conference, permitted women to sit on certain church boards and committees, but prohibited ordination of women to the pastoral ministry. It read as follows:

> 1. That the Canadian Conference of M.B. churches go on record as not favouring the ordination of women for the preaching and pastoral ministry nor their election to boards and offices whose work is of the nature of eldership, such as the Board of Spiritual and Social Concerns and the Board of Reference and Counsel or its equivalent.
>
> 2. That the Canadian Conference declare women eligible to be elected as delegates to conferences and to church and conference boards and committees other than those referred to in recommendation 1.[2]

In 1987, another resolution encouraged women to participate in specified areas of ministry. Churches were encouraged "to free and affirm women for ministries in the church, at home and abroad, in decision-making, evangelizing, teaching, counselling, encouragement, music, youth, visitation."[3] On the other hand, women could be ordained within the CMC conference, and as early as 1974, a revised resolution on ordination emphasized that efforts should be made to eliminate barriers of race, class and sex.[4] In 1987, the CMC conference committed itself to a practice of inclusiveness, involving "a growing sensitivity to our language, referring to our Christian community and our God, so that we do not implicitly exclude women."[5] In the same year, the position of president of the General Conference Mennonite Church was filled by a woman for the first time.[6]

Women were participating in decision making in the church to a greater extent than before. Author of *The History of the Canadian Women in Mission* observed: "We notice an increasing number of women participating actively in all areas of church and conference work."[7] By the mid-70s approximately one-third of delegates to the CMC Canadian conference were women.[8]

During these years, both Mennonite women and the larger Mennonite community became more affected by women's issues. Increasingly, women questioned traditional interpretations of biblical texts which had been used to support their subordination. Anna Ens referred to this in her address to the Women in Mission Annual Conference in 1982, when she said that

> we all know that there are texts that suggest subordination of women to men which have held us in bondage and that tend to hinder the implementation of God's purpose for unity and partnership in Christ's body, the church. As we have found clarity about other troublesome texts . . . so we can also find clarity about texts that, taken in isolation, on the surface suggest subjugation and silence on the part of women.[9]

Katie Funk Wiebe also emphasized the need "to disentangle biblical teaching from cultural accretions," stating that

> women in Mennonite churches will not always sit outside the inner circle of church life. The gap between what they can do and what they are allowed to do will disappear. The church will not always be afraid to give women the opportunity to develop full use of their talents of love, concern, intellect, spiritual and special skills. They will not always be considered second class citizens in the kingdom of God.[10]

In a five-part series entitled "God's Word: To Women as to Men," Hedy L. Martens examined both the original languages and cultural contexts of scriptures which had limited women's role in the church (Eph. 5:22; 1 Pet. 3:1; 1 Cor. 11, 14; 1 Tim. 2; Gen. 2:18), concluding that in the Christian church men and women are called equally to mutual submissiveness.[11] (Martens was later criticized for "twisting scripture" and liberating women beyond what women desire.)[12]

Some Mennonite women's societies were beginning to discuss women's roles. Two groups in Saskatchewan studied a Christian feminist book, *All We're Meant To Be*, "a biblical outlook to women's liberation. This has been a great blessing to all of us and we recommend this book to any women interested in a serious study of God's place for women in our world."[13]

However, while some women's societies felt the women's movement should be taken seriously,[14] others reacted against it. In 1978, a female speaker at the South Saskatchewan MB Women's Auxiliary meeting, asserted that "any lady thinking she needs to be liberated needed to hear these ladies share how they are liberated in the Lord."[15] Some groups also opposed inclusive language.[16]

Not only were issues of women's equality raised within Mennonite women's societies, they also were discussed within the broader church context in church periodicals and at conferences. Here as well, the women's movement was referred to in both negative and positive terms. Marie K. Wiens in "Full Church Citizenship for Women?" advocated a more active role for women in the church, but at the same time made it clear that her viewpoint was not due to "any women's lib tendencies, but because of a deepening awareness of the church's meaning in our lives."[17] Luetta Reimer, on the other hand, tried to clarify misunderstandings about the Women's Liberation Movement in "A Christian

Response to the Women's Liberation Movement" stating that "the general spirit of equality, justice, and personal dignity promoted by the movement is clearly compatible with Christ's teachings on human relationships."[18] In 1973, the *Mennonite Reporter* carried a four-part series on the role of women.[19] While one article in the series warned the Christian community to "avoid the traps of the radical women's liberation movement," another referred to the "consequence of generations of subtle suppression in the church," and a third discussed the issue of sexist language.[20] In a 1976 article on a male perspective of feminism, a husband of a feminist woman asserted that Christian feminism was liberating for both women and men.[21]

During this era, both the CMC and the MB churches raised the issue of inclusive language. In 1980, the CMC began to refer to the chair of their conference as "chairperson" instead of "chairman."[22] In 1983, one of the workshops held at the annual CMC conference discussed the issues of female church leadership, female images of God, and sexist language.[23] In the MB community, a resolution at the 1981 Canadian conference urged members to "avoid using sexist language that offends."[24] While it recognized "that the language of scripture reflects the patriarchal societies in which the Bible emerged," the resolution also concluded that "brother" included sister and those who use this language should not be accused of being "anti-feminist."[25] Two years later, the writer of the regular column, "Personal Opinion," in the *Mennonite Brethren Herald*, defended the generic use of "man," urging readers to "speak and write correctly" and "above all, let us not misuse words and thus tamper with the Word." He ridiculed "women's liberationists" saying, "let the uninformed faddists do their thing."[26]

Exegetical papers appeared in church periodicals on interpretation of biblical texts which had been interpreted as restrictive for women. Positions of Mennonite biblical scholars ranged from advocating continued restriction to suggesting freedom for women to use all their gifts in the church.[27] Writers stressed "abiding biblical principles" but also, "passing cultural elements which may have occasioned the teachings (of the New Testament)."[28] Revised interpretation of texts which formerly had been read as restrictive, opened up new avenues for women in the church. They felt that

> women should be encouraged and feel free to use the gifts God has
> given them to build the church. . . . This includes mission work,
> counselling, teaching Sunday School, preaching, teaching in our
> denominational schools, participation in Bible studies, voting, being
> convention representatives and board members.[29]

But the same writers were quick to add that Pauline restrictions, applied to today's culture, meant women should not accept "any militant espousal of 'women's lib,' any disruption of the marriage relationship in the name of freedom and equality."[30]

That the church, in this time period, was ambivalent about the roles of Mennonite women is evident in the messages it gave. Women were encouraged to become more actively involved in the church structure, taking positions for which they were gifted, yet they remained limited because of interpretations of so-called restrictive biblical texts. Women themselves were not agreed about their roles in the church. Influenced by the women's movement, some women who participated in Mennonite women's societies were eager to embrace equality as they discussed women's issues within their groups and suggested that interpretations of texts used to limit women's roles in the church could, in fact, have other meanings than those traditionally held. Other women, however, did not agree with the ideas advanced by "women's lib" and remained convinced that women's traditional roles should not change.

Notes

1 *Report of the Royal Commission on the Status of Women in Canada* (Ottawa: Information Canada, 1970): xii.
2 *1975 Yearbook of the Sixty-Fifth Canadian Conference of the Mennonite Brethren Church of North America* (Winnipeg: Canadian Conference of Mennonite Brethren Churches, 1975), p. 106.
3 Don Ratzlaff, "General Conference Reports: Board of Reference and Counsel," *Mennonite Brethren Herald* 26,16 (28 August 1987): 16.
4 *Yearbook: Conference of Mennonites in Canada* (Winnipeg: Conference of Mennonites in Canada, 1974).
5 "On inclusiveness in our fellowship," *Mennonite Reporter* 17 (27 July 1987): 18.
6 Ron Rempel, "Florence Driedger appointed president of General Conference Mennonite Church," *Mennonite Reporter* 17 (30 March 1987): 1-2. It should be noted that Driedger became president when the previous president died; a vote had been taken to determine whether the board would allow a woman to serve as president.
7 Hooge, *The History of the Canadian Women in Mission*, pp. 35-36.
8 *Yearbook: Canadian Conference of Mennonites in Canada*, p. 58.
9 Anna Ens, "Leadership: Christ our Model," Canadian Women in Mission 30th Conference, 3 July 1982.
10 Katie Funk Wiebe, "Woman's Freedom: The Church's Necessity," *Direction* I, 3 (July 1972): 82.
11 Hedy L. Martens, "God's Word: To Women as to Men," *Direction* V, 1 (January 1976): 11-25.
12 Shirley Bergen, "Not True to Life," and Dave Loewen, "Freedom through Submission," *Mennonite Brethren Herald* 15, 9 (30 April 1976): 8,9; Rudy Bartel, "Somewhat Uneasy," *Mennonite Brethren Herald* 15, 10 (14 May 1976): 9.
13 Bartel, *Saskatchewan Women in Mission*, p. 21.
14 Ens, "Leadership," Canadian Women in Mission 30th Conference.
15 South Saskatchewan Mennonite Brethren Ladies Auxiliary, Minutes, 1959-87.
16 This is evident in the effort made by Mennonite women to reverse the prior CMC conference decision and change the use of "chairperson" back to "chairman." See *Yearbook: Conference of Mennonites in Canada* (Winnipeg: Conference of Mennonites in Canada, 1982).
17 Marie K. Wiens, "Full Church Citizenship for Women?" *Mennonite Brethren Herald* 12, 9 (4 May 1973): 18.
18 Luetta Reimer, "A Christian Response to the Women's Liberation Movement," *Direction* III, 1 (April 1974): 172.

19 Ruth Klaassen, "The role of women (1): Keeping up with our Anabaptist sisters," *Mennonite Reporter* 3 (5 February 1973): 7; Mary Regehr Dueck, "The role of women (2): In church 'people' means 'men'," *Mennonite Reporter* 3 (19 March 1973): 7; Mary Regehr Dueck, "The role of women (3): Young maidens dare not prophesy," *Mennonite Reporter* 3 (2 April 1973): 7; and Patty Shelly, "The role of women (4): The language must be changed," *Mennonite Reporter* 4 (16 April 1973): 7.

20 Klaassen, "The role of women (1)," Dueck, "The role of women (3)," and Shelly, "The role of women (4)."

21 John F. Peters, "Christian feminism: A husband's perspective," *Mennonite Reporter* 6 (20 September 1976): 7.

22 *Yearbook: Conference of Mennonites in Canada* (Winnipeg: Conference of Mennonites in Canada, 1980), p. 88.

23 *Yearbook: Conference of Mennonites in Canada* (Winnipeg: Conference of Mennonites in Canada, 1983), p. 80.

24 *Yearbook of the General Conference of Mennonite Brethren Churches*, (Hillsboro: Mennonite Brethren Publishing House, 1981), p. 47.

25 Ibid.

26 John H. Redekop, "Sexist Language," *Mennonite Brethren Herald* 22, 22 (2 December 1983): 12.

27 John E. Toews, "The Role of Women in the Church: The Pauline Perspective," *Direction* IX,1 (January 1980): 34; Howard Loewen, "The Pauline View of Woman," *Direction* VI (October 1977): 18; Allen R. Guenther and Herbert Swartz, "The Role of Women in the Church," *Mennonite Brethren Herald* 12, 9 (4 May 1973): 4-9; and David Ewert, "The Place of the Woman in the Church," General Conference Study Conference Paper, General Conference of Mennonite Brethren Churches, May 1980, pp. 88-109.

28 Guenther and Swartz, "The Role of Women in the Church," pp. 4-9.

29 Ibid., p. 9. Both Old and New Testaments are quoted to affirm the equality of men and women. Positive reference is made to Hannah, Rebecca, Anna, Miriam, Deborah, Huldah, Mary, Mary Magdalene, Susanna, Joanna, Priscilla, Phoebe, and Philip's daughters. Gal. 3:26-28 is interpreted as a statement of the principle of equality. The so-called restrictive texts (1 Cor. 11:2-16; 14:33-36; 1 Tim. 2:8-15) are analysed at length with the conclusion that these texts should be interpreted within their own cultural context.

30 Ibid.

9

Fellowship and Spiritual Growth

Between 1970 and 1987, Mennonite women's societies placed a greater emphasis on fellowship and spiritual growth than they had formerly. This trend was reflected in the naming of their organizations, stated purposes, themes for meetings and conferences, and biblical texts chosen for mottos.

During these years, there was a significant shift in naming, both among newly organized Mennonite women's societies and among those that chose to change the names of their organizations. There was a shift from service-oriented names to names denoting fellowship. (Tables 7 and 8 include women's societies organized between 1970 and 1987 in churches established between 1874 and 1952 .)[1]

Table 7
Percentage Distribution of Names of CMC Women's Societies Organized between 1970 and 1987

CATEGORY	NAME	NUMBER	PERCENTAGE
Fellowship	Friendship Circle, Ladies Fellowship (3x), *Koinonia*	5	36
Service/Aid	Loving Deeds Ladies Group, Ladies Aid Group	2	14
Biblical Woman's Name	Dorcas Circle	1	7
Other	*Verein* (3x), The Tuesday Group, Love and Light, Evergreen Circle	6	43
TOTAL		14	100

There is a striking lack of mission/service-oriented names in the naming of these newly organized societies. Unlike the previous era, no newly organized societies between 1970 and 1987 called themselves mission groups, and only two CMC societies and one MB society had names denoting service or aid. Just as striking is the dramatic increase in names that were fellowship oriented. Whereas only 16 percent of CMC women's societies and 21 percent of MB women's societies, organized between 1953 and 1969, had names denoting fellowship (see tables 5 and 6 in Chapter 6), there was an increase to 36 percent of CMC societies and 77 percent of MB societies that were called fellowship groups between 1970 and 1987.

Not only did newly formed groups identify as fellowship groups, societies which changed their names did so as well. According to the survey of Mennonite women's societies, eleven (16 percent) of the sixty-nine CMC and fourteen

Table 8
Percentage Distribution of Names of MB Women's Societies
Organized between 1970 and 1987

CATEGORY	NAME	NUMBER	PERCENTAGE
Fellowship	Ladies Fellowship (2x), Maranatha Ladies Fellowship, Ladies Friendship Hour, Young Ladies Fellowship, Grace Fellowship, Open Door Fellowship, Women's Fellowship, *Koinonia* Fellowship	9	69
Fellowship & Service	Women's Service and Fellowship	1	8
Biblical Woman's Name	*Maria Martha Verein*	1	8
Other	Elim *Verein*, Gals with God	2	15
TOTAL		13	100

(42 percent) of the thirty-three MB women's societies, established between 1953 and 1969, changed their names between 1970 and 1987. (See table 9.)

There was a higher percentage of name changes to those denoting fellowship and Bible study than to those suggesting a service orientation. This trend was more evident among MB women's societies than among CMC women's societies; and the tendency to changes in naming to service/mission/aid was greater among CMC women's societies.[2]

As names showed a shift to a more explicit fellowship focus, women's groups also clearly stated that fellowship and spiritual growth were primary functions of their groups. The aspect of fellowship was variously referred to as friendship, spiritual fellowship, Christian fellowship, or sharing. It included both a personal element of bonding among sisters and a spiritual component. A newly organized women's society in the Vineland United Mennonite Church articulated this at their first meeting: "Our first meeting was held October 4, 1976, with fifteen present. At that meeting we held elections and decided on the name 'Friendship Circle' which is the theme and purpose of our group."[3] In 1977, the Arnaud Christian Fellowship stated that the "purpose of our Fellowship is to further each member's spiritual growth and lead us to a closer fellowship with Christ and each other."[4] The Arelee MB Women's Missionary Fellowship reported in 1982 that since "the Bible is our key to living, each time we gather we have a Bible study and a time of sharing."[5] A 1972 report of the Women's

Missionary Service of the Ontario MB Conference referred to the importance of Christian fellowship: "The aspect of Christian fellowship is emphasized at the monthly meetings where more and more time is devoted to Bible study and prayer, discussion of specific questions, and the sharing of experiences. Very real spiritual needs have been met during these meetings."[6]

Table 9
Mennonite Women's Societies' Name Changes
1970-1987

NAME CHANGE	CMC WOMEN'S SOCIETIES	MB WOMEN'S SOCIETIES	TOTAL SOCIETIES	PERCENTAGE
To Fellowship/Bible Study: Ladies Fellowship (3x), *Koinonia* Ladies Group, Women's Christian Fellowship (2x), Women's Fellowship (2x), Fellowship, Friendship Circle (2x), Ladies Bible Study Group	3	9	12	48
To Mission/Aid/Service: Ladies Aid, Willing Workers, Women's Auxiliary, Women in Mission (3x), Women's Mission Circle, Women's Ministries	6	2	8	32
To a Combination of Missions & Fellowship: Missionary Fellowship (2x)	1	1	2	8
Other Name Changes: Church Women, Women Alive, Ladies Group	1	2	3	12
TOTAL	11	14	25	100

The priority given to fellowship and spiritual growth concerns can also be noted by the fact that, after 1970, constitutions and reports of Mennonite women's societies often mentioned these before referring to goals of mission and service. At the provincial level, one example is found in the 1980 constitution of the Women's Conference of the Mennonite Brethren Church of Manitoba. The constitution stated that the aims of the Conference were "to unite the women of the churches for the purpose of promoting spiritual growth and fellowship; to assist in the various needs and programs of our conference with prayer, practical work and donations."[7] The 1976 report of the Ontario MB Women's Missionary Service likewise gave priority to fellowship in its statement of purpose: "1. promote spiritual growth and inspiration for service through the fellowship of women in our conference, and 2. help various needs of the church and conference with prayer, interest and financial support."[8] In local churches as well, accounts of women's groups gave pre-eminence to fellowship and spiritual growth. The Boissevain Women in Mission reported that "at a recent re-organizational meeting we were asked to share our reasons for attending. The reasons given were: for fellowship, to become better acquainted and to become involved in the mission of the church."[9] The same was true for the Junior Ladies Aid of Herbert MB Church, who indicated that their two-fold purpose was "a) To enjoy and practise Christian fellowship and b) To give a helping hand whenever and wherever we are able to."[10] In 1980, the Homemakers of the Dalmeny Community Church stated that their aim was "to grow in the grace and knowledge of our Lord Jesus Christ, and to put that growth into action."[11] In the same year, the Magdalene Ladies Aid in Hanley, Saskatchewan, ended their annual report with a statement of appreciation for the fellowship they had experienced in the group, as well as the opportunity "to contribute to the work of our church."[12] In all these instances, women's societies mentioned fellowship and spiritual growth before service.

Another sign of the shift to an emphasis on fellowship and spiritual growth is seen in the themes for meetings and conferences of Mennonite women's societies, and in biblical texts chosen as group mottos. Women chose to discuss issues that would encourage Christian growth. At the provincial level, Saskatchewan Women in Mission conference themes between 1972 and 1976 included "Christ as Lord of Life," "Today's Christian Woman," "Rejoice, and Again I Say Rejoice," and "Coping with Life Through the Power of the Spirit."[13] In 1971, the theme of the Women's Missionary Service of the Ontario MB Conference was "God's Woman for the 70s," and included topics such as "Understanding Myself," and "New Directions for My Life."[14] In 1984, the theme was "Be Still and Know That I Am God."[15] At the 1974 Women's Conference of Manitoba MB Churches, a physician spoke to the group on dreams, bio-feedback, crying as therapy, and communications.[16] The same trend is evident at a local level. In 1984, the Arnaud Christian Fellowship chose the theme, "Be All You Can Be."[17] In 1977, Boissevain Women in Mission decided to study the stories of biblical women during group meetings.[18] In 1982, the Ladies Aid of Main Centre, Saskatchewan, studied the book *The Fragrance of Beauty* in order "to help each woman conquer through Christ personal fear, worry, inferiority or anger which may be threatening her inward and outward beauty."[19]

Biblical texts chosen as group mottos also reflect the change in emphasis. Of the fourteen CMC and thirteen MB women's societies organized between 1970 and 1987 (see tables 7 and 8), a few specified biblical texts as mottos.[20] Texts chosen included:

> But they who wait for the Lord shall renew their strength, they shall mount up with wings like eagles, they shall run and not be weary, they shall walk and not faint. (Isa. 40:31)
> Therefore encourage one another and build one another up, just as you

are doing. (1 Thess. 5:11)

And let us consider how to stir up one another to love and good works. (Heb. 10:24)

So then, as we have opportunity, let us do good to all men, [21] and especially to those who are of the household of faith. (Gal. 6:10)

For by grace you have been saved through faith; and this is not your own doing, it is the gift of God. . . . above all taking the shield of faith, with which you can quench all the flaming darts of the evil one. (Eph. 2:8; 6:16)

But the fruit of the Spirit is love, joy, peace, patience, kindness, goodness, faithfulness. (Gal. 5:22)

For the grace of God has appeared for the salvation of all men, training us to renounce irreligion and worldly passions, and to live sober, upright, and godly lives in this world, awaiting our blessed hope, the appearing of the glory of our great God and Saviour Jesus Christ, who gave himself for us to redeem us from all iniquity and to purify for himself a people of his own who are zealous for good deeds. Declare these things; exhort and reprove with all authority. Let no one disregard you. (Tit. 2:11-15)

These choices of biblical texts indicate that the degree of emphasis on service was not as substantial as in former years; mottos reflect a shift toward concerns about personal growth. Service-oriented terms such as "good works," "do good," and "good deeds" each appear only once in biblical mottos chosen between 1970 and 1987, whereas themes of spiritual growth predominate: "they who wait for the Lord shall renew their strength," "encourage one another and build one another up," "taking the shield of faith," "the fruit of the Spirit is love," and "live sober, upright, and godly lives."

It is difficult to determine what caused the shift to an increased emphasis on fellowship and spiritual growth in Mennonite women's societies. While not many groups stated explicitly why this occurred, the report of the Happy Homemakers of First Mennonite Church in Saskatoon indicated that women had a sense that there was "a lack of growth and development in spiritual matters, and so in 1981, their perspective shifted from being a fundraising organization to a Bible study group that meets once a week for prayer and study."[22] A further indication of why this shift in emphasis occurred is noted in the opening address of the 1979 annual conference of CWM. Anne Neufeld stated that

Women in Mission speaks of action and involvement. We have been known to reach out. But to reach out effectively we need to grow inwardly. For our inward journey we need the refreshing resources that come from God through His Word (through meditation and fellowship). . . . We want to have His message so deeply rooted in our lives that it governs our thinking. This will be to us individually, and as WM corporately, joy and encouragement in our services to one another and to our sisters around the world.[23]

The concern here was to make sure that actions of service were grounded in personal spiritual experience.

Whatever the various reasons for the shift in priorities from a primary focus on support for missions to more emphasis on fellowship and spiritual growth, it is clear that a change in orientation began during this time period.

Notes

1   Documentation is from provincial histories of CMC women's societies, local church histories, and the survey.

2   One factor to keep in mind, however, is that local CMC women's societies were prone to change their name to Women in Mission after 1975, the year when the national CMC women's organization changed its name to Canadian Women in Mission.

3   John Giesbrecht et al., *Highlights of the Vineland United Mennonite Church (1936-1986)* (n.p., 1986), p. 30.

4   Froese, *Manitoba Mennonite Women in Mission (1942-1977)*, p. 22.

5   "Arelee MB Missionary Fellowship," *Arelee and District History* (N.p., 1982).

6   Mary Dueck, "Report," in *Yearbook of the Forty-First Annual Provincial Conference of the Mennonite Brethren Churches of Ontario*, (N.p.: Conference of the MB Churches of Ontario, 1972), p. 25.

7   "Constitution of the Women's Conference of the Mennonite Brethren Church of Manitoba," Women's Conference of the Mennonite Brethren Church of Manitoba, 1980.

8   Elva A. Suderman, "Women's Missionary Service Report," *Yearbook of the Forty-Fifth Annual Provincial Conference of the Mennonite Brethren Churches of Ontario* (N.p.: Conference of the Mennonite Brethren Churches of Ontario, 1976).

9   Froese, *History of Manitoba Mennonite Women in Mission (1942-1977)*, p. 25.

10 Tina Block, "Junior Ladies Aid Report," Minutes, Herbert Mennonite Brethren, Herbert, Saskatchewan, 1977, p. 20.

11 Margaret Lepp, "Homemaker's Report," Minutes, Dalmeny Community Church, Dalmeny, Saskatchewan, 1980, p. 14.

12 Helen Froese, "Report of the Magdalene Ladies Aid for 1980," Minutes, Hanley Mennonite Church, Hanley, Saskatchewan, 1980.

13 Bartel, *Saskatchewan Women in Mission*, p. 8.

14 Mary Dueck, "Women's Missionary Service of the Ontario Mennonite Brethren Conference," in *Yearbook of the Fortieth Annual Provincial Conference of the Mennonite Brethren Churches of Ontario* (N.p.: Conference of the Mennonite Brethren Churches of Ontario, 1971), p. 55.

15 Loretta Heide, "Women's Missionary Service of the Ontario Mennonite Brethren Conference," in *Yearbook of the Fifty-Third Annual Provincial Conference of the Mennonite Brethren Churches of Ontario* (N.p.: Conference of the Mennonite Brethren Churches of Ontario, 1984).

16 "Minutes of the Eighth Annual Women's Conference of the Manitoba Mennonite Brethren Churches," Women's Conference of the Manitoba Mennonite Brethren Churches, 1974.

17 Margaret Kathler, "Arnaud Christian Fellowship," Report, Arnaud Mennonite Church, 1984.

18 Froese, *History of Manitoba Mennonite Women in Mission*, p. 25.

19 Diane Unruh, "Ladies Aid Report," Minutes, Main Centre Mennonite Brethren Church, Main Centre, Saskatchewan, 1982.

20 Sources are reports of Mennonite women's societies found within histories of local Mennonite churches, the survey of Mennonite women's societies, and reports of women's groups that accompanied survey responses.

21 These texts are quoted from the Revised Standard Version of the Bible. In the 1970s and 1980s, contemporary versions of the Bible were being introduced into Mennonite churches, but the biblical language was not inclusive in these versions.

22 Patkau, ed., *First Mennonite Church in Saskatoon*, p. 198.

23 Anne Neufeld, "Canadian Women in Mission Minutes–7th Annual Conference," in *Yearbook: Conference of Mennonites in Canada* (Winnipeg: Conference of Mennonites in Canada, 1979).

10

Some Things Remain the Same

While fellowship and spiritual growth received greater emphasis between 1970 and 1987, other aspects of Mennonite women's societies remained the same. First, many Mennonite women's societies continued to have a strong biblically motivated emphasis on service. Second, regular meetings followed the same format as they had in the past; and third, participation in Mennonite women's societies still held significant meaning for women who attended.

Mission/service initiatives of Mennonite women's societies continued to be biblically inspired; women stated that their work of service was done in response to the Christian gospel. The Mission Sisters of the Niverville Mennonite Church, for example, consciously designed their 1980 report "to show how our activities have been organized in our effort to fulfil Christ's command to feed the hungry, give drink to the thirsty, welcome the stranger, clothe the naked, visit the sick, go to the prisoner (Matt. 25:35-36)."[1] In 1972, the president of the women's auxiliary of the Leamington MB Church reported that "a brief, cold report cannot reflect the enthusiasm with which our ladies work in their various ways, but it is encouraging to see our young married ladies, and our older grandmothers joining wholeheartedly in the work which we ladies feel is a labour of love for Christ."[2] In 1977, the Tabea Mission Circle in Coaldale, Alberta, stated that members considered their service as good stewardship of "the time, opportunities and talents God has given us."[3] Biblical motivation for service remained strong.

The desire to serve prompted significant support for missions and MCC through fundraising, just as it had in the past. Mennonite women's societies continued to contribute to mission projects with large amounts of money;[4] in 1972, the CWM raised $245,000, an amount that was two-thirds the figure for the total budget for the entire national body of CMC.[5] Women's societies supported mission projects of the CMC and MB churches, as well as projects of MCC.[6] The 1979-80 report of the *Missionsverein* of the Sargent Avenue Mennonite Church enumerates what was a typical list of items produced for MCC: "seventy layettes, fifty school kits, 15 Patch Baby blankets, 10 large blankets, and 35 pounds of bandages."[7] Several groups continued having mission sales and catering for church functions,[8] but in several locales, the "arena sale" began to take the place of local church mission sales.[9] These were MCC annual mission sales for which an arena or other large building was utilized. It included sale of handmade articles, food booths, and auctions. They were supported by most of the Mennonite churches in a designated area and women's groups became involved in various aspects of the sale. For example, in the Leamington area, one women's group was in charge of the *Rollkuchen* (a deep fried flat pastry) booth.[10]

Besides the commitment to service, a second constant aspect of Mennonite women's societies was the gathering for worship. Mennonite women's societies provided a context in which each member could participate and, indeed, all were encouraged to take their turns. The Missionary Prayer Band of the Central MB Church in Saskatoon reported that "we try to involve as many sisters as possible in our meetings, in choosing hymns, reading Scripture, prayer, and having special numbers in song."[11] Components of meetings included prayer, reading from the Bible, singing, a devotional talk, business, an offering, a closing prayer, and coffee. Worship format continued to be modelled after that of the institutional church, illustrated in the 1976 report of the Junior Ladies Aid of the Herbert MB Church, in which the components of their worship were listed: "Singing of two songs, Opening prayer, Thoughts and verses (also prayer requests), Devotional, Prayer Session, Minutes, Business, Offering, Prayer, Coffee."[12] The format is strikingly similar to what would appear as the order of Sunday morning worship in a church bulletin. The Senior Women's Fellowship of the Central MB Church in Saskatoon reported a similar pattern: "We always open our meetings with singing a few songs, scripture and prayer, a devotional from the Word of God and a time of sharing. We have prayer requests and then unite in prayer."[13] Likewise, the Willing Hands Ladies Aid of Yarrow, British Columbia, stated that their meetings began "with singing and prayer; followed by the reading of the minutes; business; special numbers such as: a poem, song or testimony. During our devotional, we study a book of the Bible, which has been chosen at the beginning of the year."[14]

The tendency to model meetings after those in the larger church was also seen at the provincial conference level. For example, the 1986 South Saskatchewan MB Ladies Fall Auxiliary Meeting began with a welcome and was followed by songs, invocation, special music, business, offering, special music, a speaker, and closing.[15] Not only was the format similar to the worship service in the church, but as well, speakers seemed to organize their talks in the same way as preachers did on Sunday morning. This is illustrated at the spring conference of the 1979 Women's Conference of Manitoba MB Churches where a female speaker presented five portraits of a Christian worker, based on 1 Timothy 2.[16] This is similar to the Sunday morning three-, four-, or five-point sermon.

Was this trend to continue modelling their worship experiences on those of the institutional church an indication of a continued need within Mennonite women's societies for a parallel church organization, one in which they could freely participate in all aspects of the worship? It is difficult to make a direct correlation; however, an indication of the extent to which societies functioned as a parallel church may be examined through the meaning women's societies held for Mennonite women—an area in which Mennonite women's societies remained strong between 1970 and 1987. It is evident that through participation in women's societies, Mennonite women experienced a deep sense of community as well as significant opportunities for service. This is reflected in their reports. The Missionary Circle of Mission, British Columbia, in looking back over their years of existence, stated that

> we have been aware of the Lord's presence over the years. Who can measure the worth of a circle? We have learned to plan and work together; even to fellowship together when we disagreed, and to share each other's burdens and joys. By the grace and mercy of our Heavenly Father we have grown spiritually by being part of a Missionary Circle.[17]

Mennonite women continued to see the women's society as a venue through which they could use their gifts in service to God. In her opening remarks at the 1982 Council of Boards meeting of the CMC, Anita Froese, then president of CWM, referred to the importance of the women's society in terms of opportunities for women. She stated that

> many of these women in our Mennonite circles God has given all kinds of talents, and besides the homemaking skills they are trained in administrative and organizational skills. But many of these women do not feel comfortable in the world of church and conference boards and committees. . . . Not only has this structure [Women in Mission] given women an opportunity to use their gifts and talents, but I am sure that the results of their work are noticed in the financial reports of the various boards.[18]

It was through their women's societies that the faith of Mennonite women could find expression in action. The Winkler Bergthaler Bethel Ladies Aid reported that "it has been a privilege to be part of a Ladies Aid with many opportunities to serve the Lord with gladness. It is our sincere prayer that we continue to serve Him to the best of our abilities and take our place in the ranks of Christian workers."[19]

Thus, inasmuch as Mennonite women considered women's societies as a context in which they could support one another, grow spiritually, and live out their Christian faith, their societies seemed to function as a parallel church for them.

Not only did Mennonite women's societies remain committed to support of missions and worshipping together, but during this time, the church continued to recognize and affirm the contributions of Mennonite women's societies. In fact, it appears that, between 1970 and 1987, the institutional church made a greater effort than they had in the past to acknowledge the work of Mennonite women's societies. This was done both by statements of commendation and by efforts to include them in the official church structure.

Words of commendation came to Mennonite women's societies from the church institution at local, provincial, and national levels. For instance, in their local church history book, the Bethel Church in Aldergrove, British Columbia, concluded the section on "The Women in the Church" with the following acknowledgement of the contribution of women's groups in the church:

> From a brief look at the work of our ladies' auxiliaries, we are again
> made aware that they are more than wives, mothers, homemakers and
> often wage earners. They love to serve God and seem to possess a
> special compassion for people and children in need. We can indeed be
> thankful for the contribution our women make in building God's
> Kingdom and Bethel church as a whole.[20]

At the provincial level, the 1970 Ontario Conference of MB Churches passed a
resolution commending MB women's societies for their "many hours of labour
and sacrificial giving in support of our institutions and the missions program."[21]
On the national scene, the moderator of the CMC annual conference gave
recognition to CWM before the entire delegate body in 1981, when he said to
them:

> Your service is the glue that puts stability into our church social
> functions, and your support of Mission and Service activities at home
> and abroad is the leaven around which so much of congregational
> mission work is built. I believe, in a very real sense, that you are the
> deacons of our church and conference.[22]

The church also attempted in various ways to include them in the official
church structure. Sometimes church leaders called upon women's societies to
present entire services in the local church, either on Sunday morning or at an
evening service.[23] The Laird Fellowship Group, for example, presented Mother's
Day worship services in the local church in 1975 and 1976, and a New Year's
Eve program in 1976.[24] Another way in which the church tried to include
women's societies in the church structure was to have them report annually at
local church business meetings and provincial conferences.[25] Some Mennonite
women's societies were also asked to submit audited reports of their yearly
financial income and expenditures.[26] One could view these practices in one of
two ways: either as a desire on the part of the church to value the work of
women's societies or as an effort to control them. It is difficult to determine how
women felt about these links with the church. There is evidence from some
groups that the affirmation received from the church was appreciated. The fact
that there is no indication Mennonite women saw these initiatives as intrusive
does not preclude the possibility that the church was trying to monitor women's
societies' activities and financial matters.

That attempts were being made to recognize Mennonite women's
societies was also evident in the visibility given to women's societies at the
national level and the representation they were given on church boards and
committees. In 1981, CWM was included for the first time in the installation
service of new officers for the CMC at the annual conference and, in 1982, the
CWM president was asked to present the opening devotional to the Council of
Boards meeting of the CMC. These initiatives showed that the church
recognized the women's society as an important arm of the church. In addition,

Mennonite women's societies began to have representatives on church boards. CWM requested, and consequently received, representation on several General Conference church boards for the first time in 1974. These included the Mennonite Biblical Seminary Board, the Commission for Home Ministries, the Commission on Education, and the Commission on Overseas Mission.[27] Representation on boards also occurred at the local level. In 1980, for example, Harmony Hearts of United Mennonite Church in Black Creek, British Columbia, elected one of their members to participate on the church council.[28]

With the trend among Mennonite women's societies towards an increased emphasis on fellowship and spiritual growth; continued strength of a biblical orientation, support for missions, and meaningful worship experiences; and various efforts by the church to include Mennonite women's societies in the official church structure, one would think that women's societies would continue to grow and flourish. Yet the 1970s and 1980s was an era of decline for Mennonite women's societies, the seeds of which had been sown in the late 1960s.

Notes

1 Helen Friesen, "Mission Sisters Report," Minutes, Niverville Mennonite Church, Niverville, Manitoba, 1980, p. 6.

2 Driedger, *The Leamington United Mennonite Church*, p. 125.

3 Neufeld, ed., *History of Alberta Mennonite Women in Mission*, p. 65.

4 Documentation obtained from Mennonite women's societies' financial reports which accompanied completed surveys.

5 Menno Wiebe, "Women's Conference more than peripheral," *Mennonite Reporter* 2, 15b (24 July 1972): 4.

6 Ester Patkau, *Nordheimer Mennonite Church of Saskatchewan (1925-1975)* (Hanley: Nordheimer Mennonite Church, 1975), p. 72.

7 Tina Friesen, "*Missionsverein*," Minutes, Sargent Avenue Mennonite Church, Winnipeg, Manitoba, 1979-80.

8 Bartel, *Saskatchewan Women in Mission*, pp. 67, 72.

9 Toews, ed., *South Western Ontario Women in Mission*, p. 53; Bartel, *Saskatchewan Women in Mission*, p. 91; Neufeld, ed., *History of Alberta Mennonite Women in Mission*, p. 110; Gert Dyck, "Wymark Ladies Mission Club," in *Patchwork of Memories* (N.p., n.d.), p. 873.

10 Toews, *South Western Ontario Women in Mission (1925-1987)*, p. 53.

11 Albertine Speiser, "Missionary Prayer Band," Minutes, Central MB Church, Saskatoon, Saskatchewan, 1978, p. 10.

12 "Junior Ladies Aid," Minutes, Herbert MB Church, Herbert, Saskatchewan, 1976, p. 5.

13 Elizabeth Andres, "Senior Women's Fellowship," Minutes, Central MB Church, Saskatoon, Saskatchewan, 1982.

14 Rempel, *History of B.C. Mennonite Women in Mission*, p. 91.

15 Bulletin from the South Saskatchewan Mennonite Brethren Ladies Fall Auxiliary Meeting, Regina, 1 November 1986.

16 "Spring Conference–April 21, 1979," Report of the Women's Conference of Manitoba Mennonite Brethren Churches, 1979.

17 Rempel, *History of B.C. Mennonite Women in Mission*, p. 61.

18 Anita Froese, Canadian Women in Mission President, "Opening Devotional–Council of Boards," Minutes, Council of Boards of the Conference of Mennonites in Canada, 28 January 1982.

19 Froese, *Manitoba Mennonite Women in Mission*, p. 57.

20 *Bethel Mennonite Church (1936-1980), Aldergrove, B.C.* (Altona: D.W. Friesen and sons, 1980), pp. 40-41.

21 Boldt, ed., *A History of the Ontario Conference of MB Churches*, p. 37.

22 *Yearbook: Conference of Mennonites in Canada* (1981), p. 89.

23 Rosie Sawatsky, "Ladies Aid Activities," Minutes, Oaklake Mennonite Church, Oaklake, Manitoba, 1971; and Naomi Mission Society, Constitution, First Mennonite Church, Saskatoon, Saskatchewan, 1975, p. 4.

24 Bartel, *Saskatchewan Women in Mission*, p. 45.

25 Ontario CMC women's organizations began to report to the Ontario CMC annual conference delegate body in 1973. See Toews, ed., *South Western Ontario Women in Mission*, p. 31.

26 Ibid.; Manitou Mennonite Brethren Ladies Fellowship Constitution, Manitou Mennonite Brethren Church, Manitou, Manitoba, 1981; Letter from Pleasant Point Ladies Aid, 1988; and "Ladies Aid Report," Minutes, Main Centre Mennonite Brethren Church, Main Centre, Saskatchewan, 1979.

27 *Yearbook: Conference of Mennonites in Canada* (1974), p.79.

28 Gay Wedel, "Harmony Hearts Report–1980," Minutes, United Mennonite Church, Black Creek, British Columbia, 1980.

11

The Decline

Even though participation in women's societies was still very meaningful for many Mennonite women, there was a noticeable decline in numbers and interest, caused in part by the fact that younger women no longer seemed to be attracted to membership. This phenomenon was not unique to the Mennonite community. The president of the Montreal and Ottawa Conference of United Church Women indicated that in the 1980s, 90 percent of members were over the age of fifty and only 25 percent of young women were involved.[1] The same was true in the Presbyterian Church; the vice-president of the Women's Missionary Society (Western Division) of the Presbyterian Church estimated that only 10 percent of all Presbyterian women belonged to WMS groups in the late 1980s and that most members were over the age of fifty.[2]

Between 1970 and 1987, there was a decline in the number of new Mennonite women's societies established. In comparison to the 102 societies organized during the age of flowering, only twenty-six additional societies were formed during this time period.[3] Since younger women did not seem as interested in joining women's societies as they once had been, the earlier pattern of the establishment of additional women's groups in local churches as soon as younger women were married, began to break down in the 1970s. At the same time, members were aging and thus societies became smaller in size; some groups discontinued.[4] In 1972, for example, the Altona Mennonite Ladies Auxiliary reported that "there were only five or six members present at the annual meeting and it seemed rather difficult to get younger women interested in attending."[5] This phenomenon was noted by Gladys Goering in 1980 in her story of Mennonite women's societies in the United States and Canada. She stated that "it is of grave concern that many of its members are older women whose ranks are not being filled by younger ones."[6]

Because younger women were not as eager to join Mennonite women's societies, attempts were made to integrate them. This was one of the factors responsible for the name change in 1975 from Canadian Women's Missionary Conference to Canadian Women in Mission,[7] a name which was meant to be inclusive of all women in the church. Writer Katie Hooge noted that

> women were divided in their thinking about the women's missionary associations which were part of every denomination. Some thought the time had come for all separate organizations, both male and female, to be done away with. Others felt that women's organizations ought to be one means of helping all women achieve a greater church involvement, including those who were not members of their group.[8]

Women made concerted efforts to plan meetings and events that would interest younger women. In 1973 the Canadian Women's Conference of the CMC initiated a consultation on the biblical interpretation of the role of women with the hope that more younger women would become interested in joining Mennonite women's societies.[9] The shift in some groups to discussion of social issues such as pornography, abortion, alcoholism, and child abuse,[10] was sometimes perceived as catering to the interests of younger women. In 1986, the president of CWM alluded to this in her presentation at the fiftieth anniversary of a local Mennonite women's society, when she noted that "once the highlight of the conference was report of a returning missionary. Now the older members are often bewildered by the emphasis on peace and justice issues, such as TV advertising, child abuse, war toys, and other social issues."[11] The fact that older members seemed bewildered indicates that the new emphasis on discussion of issues was not necessarily of primary interest to them, but was incorporated in an effort to encourage younger women to join.

Along with the decline in membership came a general self-questioning of the usefulness of Mennonite women's societies. In 1976, the Ontario WMS voiced questions about their organizations:

> In this day, when the validity and effectiveness of women's organizations are repeatedly questioned, we too are prompted to evaluate our activities of the past year in order to decide whether there is any justification in our monthly meetings in our respective churches or in our joint meeting at the annual rally.[12]

In Manitoba as well, the MB Women's Conference wondered about the place of women's societies vis-à-vis Jesus' command, "Go ye, therefore, and teach all nations" (Matt. 28:19). They asked:

> Where do we fit into this picture of 'Go ye'? The Lord gives this command to all Christians. You and I must find our place and get involved. Many changes have taken place in the past few years and more may take place in the future. Therefore it is very important that we as women's groups and as individuals find our involvement in today's world.[13]

While they did not specify which changes were taking place, they did consider it necessary to rethink their activities and their response to Jesus' command. The CWM was specific about what needed re-evaluation, stating that

> as society changes and the role of women evolves, so too will the activities and projects of the women's conference. Twenty-five years ago the work done by the WMA were projects of the hand: quilting, rolling bandages, knitting, etc. As we now have an urban professional group within our organization we have the capacity to be active in many new areas of social welfare, community involvement, speaking to social issues.[14]

As this excerpt indicates, women were beginning to question their traditional mode of service. In 1980, the president of a Mennonite women's society in the First Mennonite Church in Saskatoon expressed her hope that "as Women in

Mission we will not only be busy with fundraising, serving and sewing, but that there will be time to relate to the hurting and lonely and also to show love and caring for each other."[15] In her 1978 annual report, the CWM president referred to this as well, stating that

> in the past few years we have seen needs change. It is no longer practical to send overseas many items such as clothing, layettes, soap, etc., and so it has become necessary to rethink some of our activities. At the same time I think we have also become more aware that sometimes it is more important to share of ourselves than to share our material wealth with people.[16]

Several groups no longer conducted mission sales nor did they cater church-related meals.[17] Responses to the survey substantiated this trend; offerings and donations increasingly replaced sales and catering as methods of fundraising in the 1970s and 1980s.

What were the causes for these changes in Mennonite women's societies and the decline in membership? While this may be difficult to determine, women themselves have suggested several reasons, as indicated in the following excerpts:

> The fact that many women were in the workforce, had families, perhaps taught Sunday School, or served on church committees, made it more of a challenge to interest women in the Wednesday evening fellowship where they would gather to quilt, roll bandages, plan programs, or attend meetings.[18]

> Times have changed. The majority of us (approximately two-thirds) are working outside the home. Most are involved in intensive church work in addition to career and home responsibilities. We are constantly having to redefine our goals, priorities, and boundaries of service. We find we want to help in *Verein* work but energy and time are beginning to be a problem.[19]

> In recent years, we have found it more difficult to meet regularly as many ladies have become involved in full-time and part-time occupations outside of the home. However, we feel our commitment to service as women in mission has not diminished if we consider the diverse interests and involvements of our *Verein* members. Firstly, we are ladies who are busy as Sunday School teachers, Girls' Club workers, pianists, organists, handbell ringers, choir directors, and librarians. We serve on various church committees locally, as well as at the conference level; we assist in the operation of the Cancer Society, Canadian Food Grains Bank, the South Essex Community Council, and the Candy Striper program at the Home.[20]

> Many young women with families work part-time or full-time; . . . they have evening activities including study courses, or 'going out'

entertainment; . . . It seems the social need the *Verein* once provided is
not there any more. New groups do not happen spontaneously. . . .
Some members express a lack of enthusiasm and motivation in their
groups and they are discouraged. The nomination committee has
difficulty finding women willing to serve on the executive. The
attendance at our Women in Mission conference meetings has
decreased.[21]

There have been many changes in the twenty-one years that have passed
. . . many of the ladies were farmers' wives at first; since then many
husbands have changed their professions and the ladies too have joined
the ranks of the various professions, such as nurses, secretaries,
teaching, and business ventures, besides all being homemakers.[22]

Working women, women going back to school to get more education,
more community and church involvement, these are affecting attendance
and attitudes toward WMS. Is WMS in trouble? Perhaps. More likely
WMS is in the process of changing. How to change, which direction
to take, defining the purpose of a WMS today, wondering whether
younger women will carry on what has been done so far. These
questions are being discussed and must receive attention.[23]

These statements show that Mennonite women were now joining the paid
workforce in greater numbers than before, participating in the local church more
actively, volunteering in the community, pursuing their education, and fulfilling
their social needs elsewhere than in the context of the women's society. These
are all reasons given by Mennonite women for decrease in interest in
participation in Mennonite womens' societies. As Mennonites became more
acculturated to the society around them, Mennonite women, along with other
women in society, were stepping outside of the home in greater numbers.

Mennonite women were also becoming more involved in the church. As
more women began to serve as delegates to the CMC annual conference, some
questioned the value of meeting separately at the conference as women's
societies. They noted that "many of our women are delegates to the Conference
Sessions. Do we still need to meet as women only? Should we continue to run
parallel sessions . . . ? What is the future direction of Women in Mission?"[24]
Since a greater percentage of women were now delegates to the CMC, thereby
participating in the church more fully, women wondered whether their gendered
societies were still necessary. Along with increased church involvement came an
awareness of their auxiliary status vis-à-vis the church, a status which they felt
could impede mutuality between women and men in the church. They wondered
whether women's societies should "continue a separate existence, remain an
auxiliary? Must WM be dissolved to make room for greater mutuality and
partnership in the Conference?"[25]

In 1978, the question of the value of Mennonite women's societies became the focus of an entire issue of the MCC Peace Section Task Force on Women in Church and Society Report.[26] In it, Mennonite women's groups reflected on the usefulness of their organization. The following questions were to guide their thinking:

> Are they (women's organizations) able to appeal to the majority of church women? Is the zeal to proclaim the Gospel to all the world still present? If not, what has replaced it? Have church women's organizations allowed themselves to become a church within a church, happy with the fellowship and worship taking place there? Should organizations continue to serve as an auxiliary organization or has the time come to think of disbanding and working together with the others?[27]

The editorial, "Focus on the Auxiliary Syndrome," defined "auxiliary," as "a helpful but 'outside' contribution to the central core of the church. 'Help' means giving of oneself to complete or supplement another's work, task or responsibility."[28] The editor noted that Mennonite women, including leaders in Mennonite women's organizations, "have been struggling against this auxiliary image and are beginning to claim full membership in the church community, a role which includes shared involvement in setting priorities and in decision-making with regard to the entire church's ministries."[29]

One sign of women's desire for inclusion, although not common among Mennonite women's societies, was the use of inclusive language. A few women's society reports referred to their leader as "chairperson."[30] In 1985, the CWM president quoting a familiar hymn of the church, changed it to inclusive wording, from "brother" to "person": "I bind my soul this day to the person far away, And the person near at hand; in this town and in this land."[31]

If Mennonite women were questioning the usefulness of their gendered societies during this era, what kept them viable? In 1987, Anita Froese, CWM president, referred to

> an uneasiness and uncertainness among those inside and outside of Women in Mission circles. What lies ahead for Women in Mission? Is WM still essential in church and conference structure? . . . And then when the annual reports come in and I read of all the community and church activities, the interest and support for missions and all the extra dollars that flow into church and conference coffers as a result of the work and talents of our 4,000 plus members across Canada, I remain convinced that Women in Mission have a role to fulfil in the future of our total kingdom work.[32]

Even though change was in the air, women realized that they would never be able to contribute as much to the work of the church if they did not do it through their own societies. As Joan Wiebe pointed out, this was the context in which they could use their gifts most effectively: "Until that day comes when everyone feels free to serve on a congregational level, in the capacities of wherever those talents lie, our church structures will continue to suffer from malnutrition because of the rich resources that are being tapped only by our women's organizations."[33] It appears that some women did not even want to take leadership positions in the church. In her address, "Leadership: Christ our Model," Anna Ens stated that

> for many of our Christian women the lack of female leadership in the
> church has been no problem. They appeared content to leave the duties
> and leadership of religious and public life to men and did not give the
> matter further thought. They would never have seen themselves as
> deprived, unliberated or in bondage.[34]

Women tended to accept support roles. One woman's response to an article in the *Mennonite Reporter* that claimed women's societies were exploited by the church, argued that Mennonite women continue to willingly serve the church by raising money for its projects and by "pouring coffee."[35] The fact that women remained content in support roles is not surprising, since they did not have role models of female leadership and, in addition, were cautioned by the church against "taking our models for the husband/wife relationship and for the place of the woman in the church from the current feminist movement."[36] The church seemed to give women mixed messages about their expected role. Repeated endorsement was given to the continued relevance of 1 Corinthians 14 and 1 Timothy 2 "which put restrictions on the Christian woman," while at the same time churches were encouraged "to draw upon the spiritual resources found in our sisters for various ministries" including "participation in local church and conference ministries, if the local church so chooses."[37]

Some women, who were comfortable in their roles within women's societies and felt that through them they had a significant place within the church, resisted fundamental change; other women who found new opportunities for involvement in church and society seemed to vote with their feet. They questioned the usefulness of women's societies and became disinterested in membership.

Notes

1   Interview with Daphne Craig, Gloucester, Ontario, 1988.
2   Interview with Joan Sampson, Ottawa, Ontario, 1988.
3   See table 4, chapter 6.
4   Bartel, *Saskatchewan Women in Mission*, p. 92; Jennifer Banman, "Osler Mennonite Church," unpublished paper, Religious Studies course at Canadian Mennonite Bible College, Winnipeg, Manitoba, April 1982; Enns, "Ladies Fellowship Groups, Clearbrook MB Church," p. 100; Rempel, *History of B.C. Mennonite Women in Mission*, p. 64; Mary Anne Reimer, "Mission Sisters' Report," Minutes, Niverville Mennonite Church, Niverville, Manitoba, 1988, p. 15; Grace Loewen, "Ladies Fellowship Report," Minutes, Community Fellowship Mennonite Brethren, Newton, Manitoba, 1988; Katharina Thiessen, "Later Development of the Ladies' Circle," in *A History of the First Mennonite Church, Greendale B.C.*, p. 21; and *Bethel Mennonite Church*, p. 38.
5   Froese, *Manitoba Mennonite Women in Mission*, p. 19.
6   Goering, *Women in Search of Mission*, pp. 117-118.

7   Hooge, *The History of the Canadian Women in Mission*, p. 28.

8   Goering, *Women in Search of Mission*, p. 89.

9   "Minutes of the 21st Canadian Women's Conference," Canadian Women in Mission, 7 July 1973.

10 "Canadian Women in Mission 34th Annual Conference," in *Yearbook* (1986), pp. 98, 107; Anita Froese, President, Canadian Women in Mission Report, "From Anita's Desk (Report–1985)," 1985.

11 Neufeld and Peters, *Fifty Years Ebenezer Verein*, p. 59.

12 Dueck, "Report," *Yearbook of the Forty-First Annual Provincial Conference of the Mennonite Brethren Churches of Ontario*, p. 25.

13 Tina Brown, "President's Report 1973," Women's Conference of Manitoba Mennonite Brethren Churches, 1973.

14 Hooge, *The History of the Canadian Women in Mission*, pp. 35-36.

15 Froese, "From Anita's Desk (Report–1985)."

16 Margaret Ewert, "President's Report to the Canadian Women in Mission 26th Annual Conference," Report, Canadian Women in Mission, 7 July 1978.

17 Elizabeth Wall, "Missionary Prayer Band," Minutes, Central Mennonite Brethren Church, Saskatoon, Saskatchewan, 1983, p. 3.

18 Toews, ed., *South Western Ontario Women In Mission*, p. 33.

19 Ibid., p. 70.

20 Ibid., p. 72.

21 Ibid., p. 83.

22 Fiss, *The Story of Women in Mission*, p. 39.

23 Marie K. Wiens, "No national organization," *Mennonite Central Committee Peace Section Task Force on Women in Church and Society Report* 18 (February 1978): 6.

24 Hooge, *The History of the Canadian Women in Mission*, p. 30.

25 Ibid.

26 *Mennonite Central Committee Peace Section Task Force*, pp. 1-7.

27 Letter from Katie Funk Wiebe to the leaders of women's organizations in General Conference churches, 1977.

28 *Mennonite Central Committee Peace Section Task Force*, p. 1.

29 Ibid.

30 Donna Smith, "Women Alive Report," Minutes, Central Mennonite Brethren Church, Saskatoon, Saskatchewan, 1979, p. 10, and Elly Redekopp, "Ladies Sewing Circles," in *Virgil MB Church (1937-1987)*, ed. Helen Reimer Bergmann (N.p., 1987), p. 60.

31 Froese, "From Anita's Desk (Report–1985)."

32 Anita Froese, "Reflections," Report, Canadian Women in Mission, 1987.

33 Joan Wiebe, "Forum for leadership development," *Mennonite Central Committee Peace Section Task Force*, p.4.

34 Ens, "Leadership," Canadian Women in Mission 30th Conference.

35 Lydia Kehler, "Troubled about 'Women's lib' discussion," *Mennonite Reporter* 4,3 (4 February 1974): 7.

36 *Yearbook of the General Conference of Mennonite Brethren Churches*, 1981, p. 46.

37 Ibid., p. 47.

12

A Snapshot in Time

A snapshot of Mennonite women's societies in 1988 can be developed from a survey of all CMC and MB women's societies formed in churches that were established between 1874 and 1952. An analysis of survey responses will indicate whether the key dimensions that gave Mennonite women's societies their identity when they first were established still remained at the end of the 1980s. Did they still maintain a biblically based service orientation? Did the worship ritual remain constant? Did they continue to give greater priority to fellowship than to mission? Did Mennonite women still find participation in women's societies meaningful? How significant was the growing disinterest in membership?

In some ways, the identity of Mennonite women's societies in 1988 remained the same as it had been at the time of their emergence in Canada. A strong orientation of service to others prevailed; a primary focus of Mennonite women's societies at the time of their establishment in Canada. Biblical texts still informed their identity and motivation in 1988, and components of their meetings remained essentially the same as they had always been.

Survey respondents were asked to indicate, from a list of service opportunities, in which areas of service their groups were involved. These included raising money for foreign missions, visiting nursing homes, participating in World Day of Prayer, working in MCC self help stores,[1] raising money for MCC, raising money for home missions, supplying furnishings for the local church, and a category for other areas of involvement. Ninety-seven percent of CMC groups and 94 percent of MB groups specified their areas of involvement. A subsequent question asked women to indicate which projects were most important to their group. This was answered by 79 percent of CMC and 72 percent of MB groups. While survey results indicate that women's societies supported all these projects to one degree or another, figure 1 shows which projects emerged as most important for women's groups:[2]

Consistent with priorities of women's groups in the past, support for foreign missions, home missions, and MCC remained the most important avenues of service for both CMC and MB Mennonite women. These three areas combined were mentioned as priorities by 81 percent of CMC Mennonite women's societies and 74 percent of MB women's groups. Less than 10 percent of societies identified visiting nursing homes, supporting the World Day of Prayer, or supplying furnishings for the local church as the most important priorities of service. The 10 percent of CMC women's society responses and 7.5 percent of MB responses in the "Other" category included ministering to the sick in local churches and participating in community outreach opportunities, such as food hampers for the needy. Survey results pointed to a continued service

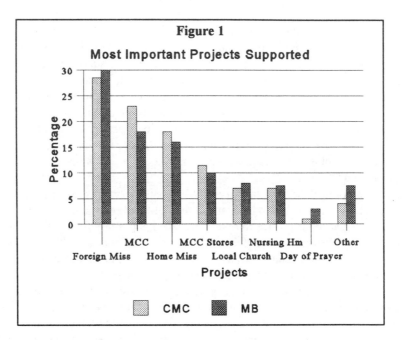

orientation within Mennonite women's societies in 1988, as well as an emphasis on biblical texts, as motivation for service.

Respondents were asked to name biblical texts that either functioned as mottos for the group or as a basis for their group's purpose and choice of projects. Forty MB groups (56 percent) and seventy-nine CMC groups (69 percent) identified biblical texts. (See table 10.)

Mennonite women in 1988 still found their impetus for service from the Bible. Seventy-three percent of biblical texts cited by CMC societies and 75 percent of MB texts referred to service (including texts with a service orientation and texts linking service to working for God). The most frequently quoted text, mentioned by eighteen groups, was Gal. 6:9,10: "and let us not grow weary in well-doing, for in due season we shall reap, if we do not lose heart. So then, as we have opportunity, let us do good to all men, and especially to those who are of the household of faith." Ever since the early years of Mennonite women's societies in Canada, this text had been a favorite motto. It shows an orientation of service to others, one that was also emphasized in the institutional church. Mennonite women's societies provided a structure whereby the passion to be faithful to God in service could find expression. In addition, the text gave Mennonite women assurance that their work would not be in vain, "for in due season we shall reap, if we do not lose heart." They needed to be convinced that their work was important, especially in the light of the feeling they sometimes had that the church did not value their contribution.

Table 10
Biblical Texts Identified by Women's Societies[3]

TEXTS	PERCENTAGE CMC SOCIETIES	PERCENTAGE MB SOCIETIES
With a service orientation	36.5	32.5
Linking service to working for God	36.5	42.5
Referring to spiritual growth	23	20
On human relationships	4	5
TOTAL	100	100

Other New Testament texts were also chosen for group mottos. Col. 3:16-17 was selected by six groups: "Let the word of Christ richly dwell within you, with all wisdom, teaching and admonishing one another with psalms and hymns and spiritual songs, singing with thankfulness in your hearts to God. And whatever you do in word or deed, do all in the name of the Lord Jesus, giving thanks through him to God the father." 1 Cor. 3:9 was mentioned five times: "for we are God's fellow workers; you are God's field, God's building." Other texts chosen refer to "supplying the needs of the saints" (2 Cor. 9:12); "deeds of kindness and charity" (Acts 9:36); "serving one another" (1 Pet. 4:10); and being "generous and ready to share" (1 Tim. 6:18). Not only did Mennonite women select biblical texts which mentioned service, they also chose those which linked acts of service to God's work, seen in phrases such as, "serve the Lord" (Ps. 100:2); "do your work heartily as for the Lord" (Col. 3:23); "serve him (God) in sincerity and truth" (Josh. 24:14); and "always abounding in the work of the Lord, knowing that your toil is not in vain in the Lord" (1 Cor. 15:58).

The fact that 27 percent of texts chosen by CMC women's societies and 25 percent by MB societies did not refer to service but to spiritual life and human relationships may be a further indication of the recent trend in Mennonite women's societies to emphasize spiritual growth and fellowship. However, biblical texts referring to service still predominated in 1988. Mennonite women continued to believe their work was done as service for God.

Components of society meetings also remained part of the snapshot of 1988. The survey listed ten possible components of society meetings: Scripture reading,[4] prayer, singing, Bible studies,[5] devotionals,[6] study of religious books, offering,[7] eating, crafts, discussion of issues, and a category for other elements. Respondents were asked to indicate which of these formed part of their gatherings. They could check as many items as pertained to their group. (See table 11.) Scripture reading, prayer, singing, a devotional, offering and eating were mentioned by more than 75 percent of both CMC and MB women's groups. These key elements, important right from the time of the emergence of Mennonite women's societies, still were part of their worship in 1988. The components of society meetings continued to resemble the format of worship services of the Mennonite church, which usually included prayers, scripture reading, singing, a sermon, and an offering. (Eating together as a community was also important to the larger church, periodically occurring in the form of potluck meals or church suppers.) Therefore, meetings of Mennonite women's societies remained modelled on the pattern of local church services.

In the "snapshot" of Mennonite women's societies in 1988, a picture has emerged that is consistent with their initial identity. They kept a service orientation based on the biblical text and their worship meetings continued to contain the same primary components they always had. Besides this, shifts in emphasis, already alluded to, continued to develop.

A gradual shift, beginning in the 1960s was that women's groups began to change their names to those denoting fellowship, with MB women's societies doing so to a somewhat greater extent than CMC women's societies.

Table 11
Components of Meetings of Mennonite Women's Societies

COMPONENTS OF MEETINGS	PERCENTAGE CMC SOCIETIES	PERCENTAGE MB SOCIETIES
Scripture Reading	92	86
Prayer	96	99
Singing	88	77
Devotional	83	81
Offering	88	90
Eating	91	80
Discussion of Issues	74	50
Bible Studies	30	57
Crafts	41	26
Study Religious Books	15	19
Other[8]	54	47

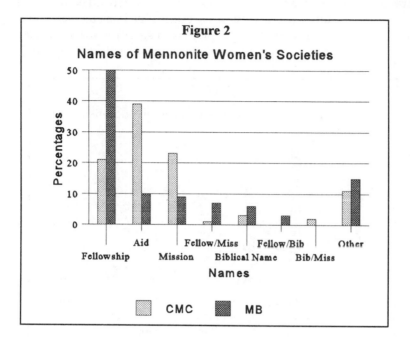

Figure 2

Names of Mennonite Women's Societies

An examination of the names and purposes of Mennonite women's societies in 1988 indicate the extent to which an emphasis on fellowship continued. For the purpose of analysis, names of societies in 1988 have been divided into eight categories: mission, aid, fellowship, biblical names, a combination of fellowship and biblical names, a combination of fellowship and mission, a combination of biblical names and mission, or a designation other than those listed on the survey. As figure 2 indicates, the trend to identify as fellowship groups continued in 1988.

Survey responses indicated a significant difference between CMC and MB naming patterns. The tendency toward fellowship names was greater in MB groups than in CMC groups, with 50 percent of MB names denoting fellowship, compared to 20 percent of CMC names. On the other hand, 62 percent of CMC groups, compared to only 19 percent of MB groups, identified themselves as mission or aid societies. Thus, in 1988, there is a greater incidence among MB women's societies of names denoting fellowship and among CMC women's societies of names exemplifying service.[9]

We can also examine the statements of purpose of Mennonite women's societies to see if these corroborate the greater tendency among MB women's societies to emphasize fellowship. The survey requested respondents to indicate the purposes of their groups. Five were suggested: fellowship, friendship and support; service to the local church; discussion of contemporary issues of

particular interest to women; evangelism; and missions. The survey asked
societies to rank their groups' purposes in order of their importance. If groups
had purposes other than those listed, they could specify it in a sixth category,
"Other." The following graph shows all the purposes with which women's

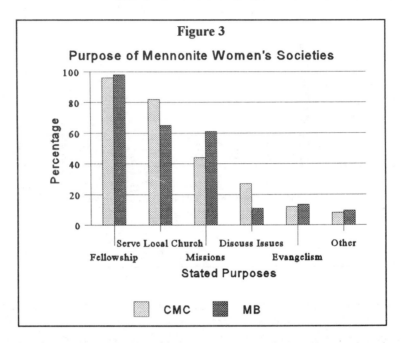

Figure 3

Purpose of Mennonite Women's Societies

groups identified. Fellowship emerged as the most frequently mentioned group
purpose with 96 percent of CMC and 98 percent of MB women's societies
stating it as a purpose of their society. Eighty-two percent of CMC and 65
percent MB groups saw service to the local church as important functions of
their group; 41 percent of CMC and 61 percent of MB groups said that an
important group focus was missions. Thus, even though MB women's societies
more frequently identified as fellowship groups by their names, when asked to
state their groups' purposes, CMC women's societies mentioned fellowship
almost as frequently as did MB societies. A difference emerged in the priorizing
of purposes. Figures 4 and 5 indicate first, second, and third priorities of
purpose for CMC and MB women's societies.

      Fellowship emerged as the most important priority of purpose for both
CMC and MB societies. The tendency for MB women's societies to stress
fellowship more than CMC societies (illustrated by the fact that 86 percent of
MB groups said that fellowship was their most important purpose compared to
64 percent of CMC groups) is consistent with the earlier discovery in naming;
more MB women's societies than CMC women's societies identified as
fellowship groups.

Reports of women's societies, submitted along with completed surveys, corroborate the importance given to fellowship. The 1988 report of the Ladies

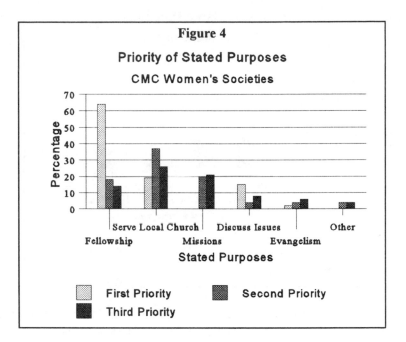

Fellowship of the Parliament MB Church in Regina, Saskatchewan, for example, listed fellowship goals before others. Their goals were:

1. To encourage friendship and fellowship between ladies.
2. To provide a prayer chain that will encourage women to pray for one another.
3. To provide an avenue of service for the ladies within our church.
4. To provide outreach to our friends and neighbours.
5. To promote an awareness of missions and to encourage our missionaries through cards, letters, gifts and prayers.[10]

Constitutions of MB groups also reflect this emphasis. The constitution of the Southern MB Ladies Fellowship stated its purpose as follows:

> The purpose of the Southern MB Ladies Fellowship shall be to provide an opportunity for spiritual fellowship and receive financial contributions from participating groups and individuals which shall be used in the support of MB missions projects.[11]

In light of the fact that support for missions was so prominent a purpose in the early years, it is noteworthy that neither denomination placed missions as their first priority. However, as indicated in figures 4 and 5, service to the local church and missions emerged as significant second and third priorities among both CMC and MB women's societies. Goals of fellowship, service to the local

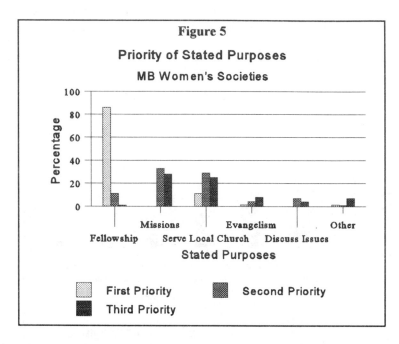

Figure 5
Priority of Stated Purposes
MB Women's Societies

church, and missions emerged as most important for Mennonite women's societies in 1988, while additional purposes, such as discussion of issues, evangelism, and those in the "Other" category[12] were not mentioned as often.

Besides the trend to emphasize fellowship, fundraising was another continuing trend, one which began in the 1960s. As noted earlier, methods of raising money for projects was beginning to shift from auctions, bake sales, bazaars, and catering to requesting cash donations. The trend to emphasize fundraising through donations continued into 1988.

Survey respondents were asked to indicate which methods of the seven enumerated (church dinners,[13] auctions, bazaars, donations,[14] bake sales, fashion shows, and garage sales) had been used in their group in 1988 and which of these were most important to them. An "Other" category was provided for listing additional methods of fundraising not included in the survey.[15] Ninety-five percent of CMC groups and 96 percent of MB groups identified their methods of fundraising.   Seventy-four percent of CMC groups and 64 percent of MB groups priorized their methods.

Figure 6 shows all the methods of fundraising used by Mennonite women's societies in 1988. The most frequently mentioned method of fundraising for both denominations was that of cash donations, with 92 percent of CMC and 93 percent of MB women's societies identifying it as one of their methods. This significant shift from the early years of fundraising, through sale of handmade articles reflects the changing identity of Mennonite women. As they became more integrated into Canadian society, as their role within the church expanded, and as they began working outside the home, they did not have as much spare time for the labor intensive activities. It was easier to contribute cash.

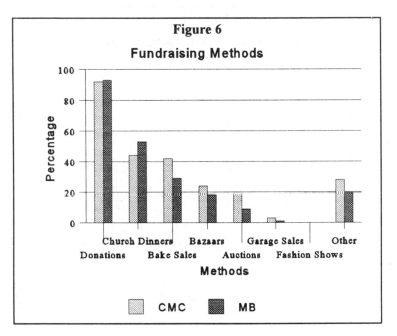

Although now the trend was to raise money through donations instead of serving food and sewing, fundraising through serving meals was still mentioned by 44 percent of CMC and 53 percent of MB groups. Bake sales were cited as fundraising events by 42 percent CMC and 29 percent MB women's groups. When respondents were requested to identify their most important methods of fundraising, over half of women's societies indicated that their most important method was through donations. Figure 7 shows the distribution of priorized fundraising methods. Fifty-one percent of CMC and 57 percent of MB groups indicated that raising money through donations was their most important method of fundraising. The method of second highest importance was preparing and serving church dinners, identified by 32 percent of CMC and 35 percent of MB groups. The 1988 financial report of the Mennonite Senior Ladies Aid in Carrot River, Saskatchewan, illustrate that women's groups used both methods of fundraising:

<u>Credits</u>
Offerings	1,169.28
Donations	100.00
Memberships	59.16

Christmas Supper   <u>112.00</u>
                                    1440.44[16]

In this case, money collected by donations and offerings far exceeded income

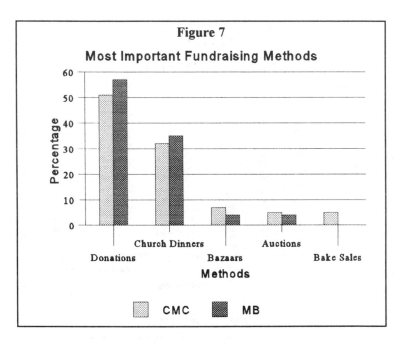

Figure 7

Most Important Fundraising Methods

from serving a Christmas supper. Money received through catering represented 7 percent of the total income while money raised by donations and offerings was 88 percent of all monies received.

     In addition to the trends to emphasize fellowship and to raise money through donations, another trend, consistent over time, was the fact of declining interest in women's societies. Survey responses and letters verified the decreasing interest of younger women in Mennonite women's societies and the fact that fewer new societies were being organized. First, society meetings were held less frequently. Survey responses indicated that only seven groups met weekly in 1988. Sixty-nine percent of CMC and 46 percent of MB women's groups met only once a month. The rest said they met every two or three weeks.

     A second indication of less interest in Mennonite women's societies was seen in the continued difficulty to involve young women. One woman wrote that "younger women do not attend because they do not feel the same need for fellowship."[17] One survey question asked respondents to indicate the age of members within Mennonite women's societies in 1988. This was answered by 90 percent of CMC groups and 92 percent of MB groups. Survey responses indicated that 67 percent of women in CMC societies and 57 percent in MB societies were over the age of fifty in 1988. However, MB women's societies had a higher percentage of members in the twenty to forty age group than did CMC women's societies (27 percent of MB members as compared to 17 percent of CMC members). Could the fact that more young MB women seemed to be joining societies than CMC women be related to greater opportunities for CMC women in the church? Young CMC women might have been attracted to other areas of church participation that were open to them. Young MB women, because they did not have the same opportunities as CMC women to participate within the institutional church, may have been more interested in joining women's societies, since that was the only church context in which they could be full participants.

In 1988, women filled eighteen percent of positions on national CMC boards and committees and 31 percent of positions on provincial CMC boards and committees.[18] In the Canadian MB church, percentages were much lower; only 7 percent of board members were women.[19] In the area of pastoral leadership, 6 percent of pastors in CMC churches were women, over half of which were either co-pastors or assistant pastors.[20] Among the MB, the percentages are again considerably lower, with only 3 percent of pastors being women.[21] Fewer women in the MB church were pastors, nonetheless, women were encouraged to use their gifts in the church. A 1988 article in the Canadian MB periodical supported the idea of husband and wife pastoral teams. It stated that

> in the secular world, on TV talk shows, news broadcasts, etc., we invariably see a man and a lady host together. In Christian telecasting it may not be a husband and wife team, but the stage is shared by both sexes. Women expect this in an age when they have equal education. It is certainly not uncommon in several other denominations in our land.
> . . . I believe most women in our churches would cheer their pastors if they shared more of their public ministry with their wives![22]

The fact that few MB women are in church leadership positions today shows that this opinion was not an opinion of the majority of MB members, and could help to explain why there were more younger women in MB women's societies than in those of the CMC.

The survey asked respondents to indicate the ages of members employed outside the home. Sixty-four percent of CMC societies and 58 percent of MB societies answered the question on employment. Survey responses show that 26 percent of CMC and 21 percent of MB members of Mennonite women's societies were employed outside the home. Of these, 62 percent of women in CMC societies who were employed outside the home were between ages forty and sixty; 63.5 percent of women in MB societies who were employed outside the home were between ages thirty and forty. If the relative decline of societies is due in part to greater opportunities to participate in church life generally, the fact of less decline in recruitment of young employed MB women would be consistent with the relatively slower pace among MBs to incorporate women in church leadership positions and, therefore, the need for their own organization.

A third indication of decline is seen in the numbers of groups that had discontinued by 1988. Eighteen CMC women's societies and thirteen MB women's societies listed groups that no longer existed; of these, six groups had discontinued in 1988.

In the light of these changes, it is important to ask whether there were also significant changes in the meaning that involvement in women's societies held for Mennonite women. What did it mean for Mennonite women to participate in Mennonite women's societies in 1988? By this time, the significance of membership was not as straightforward as it had been in the years of establishment when it was clear that Mennonite women formed societies in order to support missions and to enjoy fellowship with one another. At that time, membership meant an opportunity to serve God and to meet with other women for friendship and support. As Mennonite women became more involved, both within the Mennonite church and in society, membership in women's societies was not as weighted as heavily as it had once been. Mennonite women had more opportunities for involvement both within and outside the church. No longer was the Mennonite women's society the only outlet for service and means of support for Mennonite women.

The survey requested respondents to indicate which involvements outside of Mennonite women's society membership from the enumerated list (church sponsored Bible studies,[23] neighborhood Bible studies,[24] church sponsored mother's clubs,[25] and church fellowship groups[26] and activities related to personal development such as swimming, aerobics, and night school classes) had affected participation in these societies. An "other" category was provided for listing activities not included in the survey question. Forty-seven percent of CMC women's societies and 39 percent of MB societies reported that other involvements had lowered their attendance. Table 12 shows the percentage distribution of activities considered responsible.

Thirty-two percent of CMC women's societies and 53 percent of MB societies that answered the question, said that other religious involvements (church sponsored Bible studies, neighbourhood Bible studies, church sponsored mother's clubs, church fellowship groups) were responsible for lowered attendance in women's societies. In the "other" category women included religiously related involvements such as singing in church choirs and accepting local church positions of leadership. One group mentioned that involvement in church fellowship groups was now giving women the social interaction they needed.[27] The same group indicated that because women now were members of church committees and were deacons in the church, this provided the necessary outlet for women's participation, thus making participation in women's groups less necessary.[28] In both the CMC and the Canadian MB churches, although to a lesser degree in MB churches, women were becoming more visible in church leadership roles and had more opportunity than before to sit on church boards

Table 12
Activities Responsible for Lowered Attendance

ACTIVITY	PERCENT CMC WOMEN'S SOCIETIES	PERCENT MB WOMEN'S SOCIETIES
Church sponsored Bible studies	8%	20%
Neighbourhood Bible studies	10%	15%
Church sponsored mother's clubs	2%	9%
Church fellowship groups	12%	9%
Personal development activities	31%	22%
Other activities	37%	25%

and committees. Not only were Mennonite women beginning to participate to a greater extent in the church, but according to survey results, they were becoming more involved in activities outside of the church.

One factor that has contributed to the acculturation of Mennonite women to Canadian society is the fact that Mennonites had been gradually changing their primary language from German to English. In most Mennonite churches, the transition from the use of the German language to English began to take place in the 1960s.[29] Not surprisingly, the same phenomenon occurred in Mennonite women's societies. The survey asked respondents to indicate whether their meetings were conducted in English or German. Ninety-eight percent of CMC societies and 97 percent of MB societies answered the question. Eighty-two percent said they used either English or a combination of English and German at their meetings. A subsequent question asked which year a change in language took place. Of the 26 percent of CMC and MB groups that indicated the year in which the language of meeting changed to English, almost half of them made the changes in the 1960s, but 33 percent of those who identified the year of change said it occurred between 1970 and 1987.

The change to the English language also found expression in society name changes from German to English. Whereas until 1952, 43 percent of names of CMC women's societies and 53 percent of MB societies were German names (see tables 2 and 3 in Chapter 4), by 1988 only 11 percent of CMC and 12 percent of MB societies had German names. The language change meant that women could be involved in activities outside the home and church to a greater extent than before, since language was no longer a barrier.

As Mennonite women became more integrated into Canadian society, they were more likely to participate in activities outside of the church. In the survey question that requested respondents identify involvements that had affected attendance at society meetings, 31 percent of CMC and 22 percent of

MB societies indicated that activities geared to one's own personal development were responsible for decreased attendance (see Table 12). In addition, the "other" category identified involvements outside the church, such as women outside the home, volunteering for children's school activities, and participating in community organizations.

Employment of women outside the home was already noted as one of the reasons for decline of participation in Mennonite women's societies. As indicated earlier, 26 percent of CMC and 21 percent of MB members of women's societies were employed outside the home in 1988. This percentage is much lower than the percentage of all Mennonite women employed. In a 1989 church member profile, it was found that 56 percent of Mennonite women in Canada and the United States were employed.[30] The fact that a lower percentage of Mennonite women who were members of women's societies were employed than the percentage of all Mennonite women employed adds to the evidence that employment may be a factor in the decline of Mennonite women's societies, as indeed Mennonite women themselves have acknowledged.

With the greater integration of Mennonite women both into the larger church and society generally, it is not surprising that the identity of Mennonite women's societies was changing. The fulfilment of the religious and social needs of Mennonite women was no longer met only in the context of women's societies. Thus, the primary focus of Mennonite women's societies no longer needed to be limited to the support of mission projects and fellowship among sisters. The late 1980s witnessed the beginning of what could evolve into a refocusing of Mennonite women's societies in the future. This was the growing importance of discussion of contemporary issues at society meetings. Respondents listed topics of discussion that were common in their groups. Among them were the abortion issue, abuse, pornography, nutrition, raising children, mental and physical health, women in other countries, women in the church, pregnancy distress, day care, mothering, depression, stress, old age and death.

Although discussion of issues did not emerge as one of the three most important stated purposes of Mennonite women's societies (see figures 3, 4, and 5), 74 percent of CMC societies and 50 percent of MB societies indicated that this was a component of their meetings (see Table 11). In a subsequent survey question respondents were asked to priorize the three most important elements of their meetings; 97 percent of CMC societies and 64 percent of MB societies did so. Figure 8 shows that discussion of issues in Mennonite women's societies was beginning to emerge as an important element of meetings for a few groups. Prayer, devotionals, and discussion of issues were the most frequent elements of meetings. It does not surprise us that prayer and devotionals were key aspects of meetings, but the fact that discussion of issues ranked higher than scripture reading is perhaps an indication of a shift in focus within a few Mennonite women's societies.

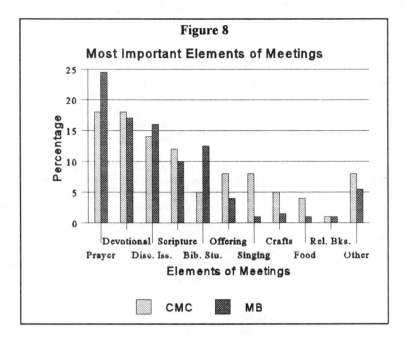

Figure 8

Most Important Elements of Meetings

The picture of Mennonite women's societies in 1988 has become clear. In some ways their identity remained the same as it always had been. The primary focus of Mennonite women's societies when they were first established, that of support of missions, remained an important focus for women's societies in 1988. This is corroborated by the CWM report at the 1988 annual CMC conference, that continued to affirm the women's society as a forum for serving God by raising money for mission projects: "Fundraising is an important aspect of WM work. . . . We are the Women in Mission. Like our counterparts in scripture we serve with vigour and enthusiasm, with courtesy and kindness, with love and compassion, making Christ known throughout the world."[31] As in the past, their service orientation continued to be based on the biblical text and components of meeting remained the same. The emphasis on fellowship and the tendency to raise money primarily through cash donations continued and grew even more prominent.

While these elements of their identity remained the same, survey responses indicated that Mennonite women's societies were no longer the only context in which Mennonite women chose to serve others and have their own needs of fellowship met. They were gradually becoming more involved in the church on church boards and committees; as deacons and church leaders; and in church sponsored groups. Yet, in spite of the relative decrease in attendance in women's societies, there remained, in 1988, a substantial number of CMC and

MB women who still found considerable meaning through their involvement in viable Mennonite women's societies in Canada.

Notes

1   In the 1960s and 1970s, stores operated by MCC were set up in numerous cities and towns across Canada in order to sell the handwork of people in developing countries as well as used clothing. These were staffed by volunteers from Mennonite churches, invariably by Mennonite women who were members of Mennonite women's societies.

2   The percentages given in this and all subsequent graphs are based on the number of women who answered each survey question.

3   Biblical texts cited in survey responses were analyzed inductively. Texts which simply referred to service, without making any connections between service and God were included in the designation "Texts with a service orientation." Pro. 31:20 is an example: "She extends her hand to the poor; and she stretches out her hands to the needy." The second category in Table 9, "Texts linking service to work for God," includes texts such as "Serve the Lord with gladness; come before him with joyful singing." (Ps. 100:2) "Texts referring to spiritual growth" included such texts as Phil. 4:4–"Rejoice in the Lord always; again I will say, rejoice." In the last category, "Texts on human relationships," were those such as Matt. 25:23: "Therefore, however you want people to treat you, so treat them, for this is the law and the prophets."

4   Scripture reading refers to reading texts from the Bible.

5   These are systematic studies of biblical texts.

6   Devotionals are talks with religious content and for Mennonites are usually based on biblical texts.

7   This is the opportunity during the meeting to contribute of one's financial resources.

8   Only 22 percent of responses in the "other" category qualified for components of meetings. These included quilting, sharing concerns, and hearing guest speakers. The remaining responses fell into the area of projects supported and included support for MCC and catering for church meals.

9   As the graph indicates, a small percentage of names were combinations of fellowship, Biblical names, missions, or aid. Names in the "other" category included names such as Homemakers, Study Group, Feminine Focus, Church Women, Harmony Hearts, Love and Light Ladies, and Evergreen Circle.

10 Betty Russell, "Ladies Fellowship," Report, Ladies Fellowship, Parliament MB Church, Regina, Saskatchewan, 1988.

11 "Constitution of the Southern Saskatchewan Mennonite Brethren Ladies Fellowship," Southern Saskatchewan Mennonite Brethren, Spring Meeting 1988.

12 Purposes in the "other" category included prayer, community service, and support for MCC.

13 The category of "church dinners" included all the money collected through serving food to larger groups, such as at weddings, graduations, congregational meals, anniversaries, and funerals.

14 This category included offerings taken at various events.

15 Of the seven methods, no one identified fashion shows and only four stated that funds were raised through garage sales.

16 "Financial Report," Mennonite Senior Ladies Aid, Carrot River, Saskatchewan, 1988.

17 Verna Heinrichs to Gloria Neufeld Redekop, Manitou, Manitoba, 1988.

18 *Yearbook: Conference of Mennonites in Canada* (1988), pp. 7-10; and Janice Hershberger, ed., *Handbook of Information* (Newton: General Conference Mennonite Church, 1988), pp. 100-110.

19 *Yearbook of the Canadian Conference of Mennonite Brethren Churches* (Winnipeg: Canadian Conference of Mennonite Brethren Churches, 1988). pp. 160-165.

20 Hershberger, ed., *Handbook of Information*, pp. 14-24.

21 Herb Kopp. ed., "The Mennonite Brethren Church in Canada: A Century of Grace," *Mennonite Brethren Herald* 27,11 (27 May 1988):2-72.

22 Mary Fehr, "Husband and wife ministry," *Mennonite Brethren Herald* 27,3 (5 February 1988):2.

23 These are Bible studies held in the local church, usually open to both women and men.

24 These are Bible studies held in a home in one's neighborhood, usually attended by women only. They are not sponsored by the local Mennonite church, but rather by an outside religious organization. Nonetheless, they served a spiritual function for Mennonite women who participated.

25 Meetings for women with young children, sponsored by the local Mennonite church.

26 Sometimes the church membership is divided into small groups of members and these groups meet periodically for discussions, studies, and fellowship. They are open to both women and men.

27 As stated by the Servettes, Mennonite women's society in the Waterloo/Kitchener Mennonite Church, Ontario.

28 Ibid

29 Toews, *A History of the Mennonite Brethren Church*, p. 329 and Samuel F. Pannabecker, *Open Doors: The History of the General Conference Mennonite Church* (Newton: Faith and Life Press, 1975), pp. 173-174.

30 J. Howard Kauffman and Leo Driedger, *The Mennonite Mosaic: Identity and Modernization* (Scottdale: Herald Press, 1991), p. 115. Two member profiles were conducted by these authors, one in 1972 and another in 1989. Since the latter is the closest to the year of our survey, figures from this profile were used in determining the number of all Mennonite women employed. A cautionary note regarding the representativeness of the profile with respect to CMC and Canadian MB women is that the survey sample included five Mennonite and Brethren in Christ denominations in Canada and the United States. However, General Conference Mennonites and the MB comprised half of the participating congregations.

31 *Yearbook: Canadian Conference of Mennonites in Canada*, 1988, p. 107.

13

Where To?

Today, while many Mennonite women are still eager participants in women's societies, disinterest in membership, especially among younger women, remains a concern. As a result, Mennonite women's societies are wrestling with the question of how to proceed. At the same time, women are finding additional avenues of opportunity within the church setting and the larger church institution is being challenged to become more inclusive of women.

Mennonite women's societies have retained their emphasis both on fellowship and the support of missions. Recently, it was reported that CMC women's groups in Ontario gathered for their 1995 annual meeting, "seeking spiritual nourishment and the peace of communing with one another."[1] Missions also remain an important focus for women's societies. At the fifty-sixth annual B.C. Women in Mission Conference on April 30, 1995, one of the leaders stated it this way: "If there is one single thread woven through the early years of women's groups in B.C., it is the determination of Mennonite women to network with each other and be part of the mission of the church."[2] Speakers at both the Saskatchewan and Manitoba 1995 annual Women in Mission conferences, were women who had been working for the church in an overseas assignment.[3] At a Women in Mission conference in Ontario in 1992, the president encouraged women "to be ready to serve, and be mission-minded mentors to our seniors, daughters and granddaughters."[4] The emphasis at these conferences underlines the interest of Mennonite women's societies in continuing to support mission work.

The decline of Mennonite women's societies continued into the 1990s. In July of 1995, at the annual CMC conference, the CWM sponsored a workshop entitled, "Demise or Rebirth." The workshop sought to address the dilemma faced by Mennonite women's societies today, whether or not they should continue to function despite declining interest. The difficulty attracting younger women to join women's societies was seen as the reason for the fear of demise.[5] In the recent celebration of the fiftieth anniversary of the Bethel Mennonite Church Women in Mission group in Winnipeg, Manitoba, one member of the group hoped that "the day will come when all women, young and old, will feel it their duty to be a part of Women in Mission."[6] At the end of the evening, which included a meal together, the youngest woman at each table was given the floral centerpiece to take home; a symbol of the importance of younger women in the group.

The decreasing interest in Mennonite women's societies by younger women has meant a decline in the number of Mennonite women's groups in Canada. In Saskatchewan, for example, there were sixty-six CMC Women in

Mission groups with 1,196 members in 1977, but in 1994, only forty-nine societies with seventy-five members.[7] In Alberta, CMC women's societies increased from nine groups and eighty-eight members in 1947 to nineteen societies with 356 members in 1977, but by 1991, enrolment dropped to eleven groups with 209 members.[8] Alberta Women in Mission felt that the reality of decline was important enough to devote a good part of a recent annual meeting to a discussion about declining membership and options for the future. After the meeting, they passed a resolution calling for a study of the question of the future of Alberta Women in Mission prior to making a decision in 1996 regarding its continued existence.[9]

Though the reasons women give for decline in the 1990s remain primarily the same as in the previous two decades, there are additional factors. Reasons that continue to dominate are that they are too busy; "many women are in the work force, some are studying."[10] Another contributing factor, already identified by survey respondents in 1988, is the tendency for women to join small groups in the local church other than the traditional women's society group. These include groups for mothers with small children, Bible study groups, and fellowship groups of women and men. But there is, perhaps, another reason why attendance in Mennonite women's societies is declining. This has to do with an increase in opportunities for women within the larger church institution.

Several initiatives, begun in the 1990s, have allowed for Mennonite women to dialogue with each other in settings other than the official church and other than within the context of women's societies. The first initiative was a conference, sponsored jointly by Mennonite Central Committee Canada Women's Concerns and by Conrad Grebel College in Waterloo, Ontario, entitled "In a Mennonite Voice: Women Doing Theology." The conference was organized in order "to provide a forum for Mennonite women to work on theological issues and to provide a meeting place for women and men who are interested in exploring the emerging theological voices of women."[11] Papers to be presented were published in advance in the *Conrad Grebel Review* periodical. The second "Women Doing Theology" conference entitled, "Mennonite Voices in Dialogue," was held in 1994. Both conferences provided opportunity for a diversity of women, including women who are members of Mennonite women's societies, together with several men, to dialogue about issues important to women. These included topics such as "Mennonite Women Connecting Faith and Practice," "Women's History–Women's Theology: Theological and Methodological Issues in the Writing of the History of Anabaptist-Mennonite Women," "Towards a Mennonite Feminist Approach to the Bible," "The Pleasure of Our Lives as Text," "Atonement," "Forgiveness," and "New Vision for Anabaptist Feminism." A third women's theological conference, "Wind and Fire," took place in May 1996. These conferences have allowed Mennonite women to "do theology" themselves and to join a community of other Mennonite women whose desire it is to formulate and own their own theology.

In addition to these theological conferences, the first academic conference on Anabaptist Women's History was held in Lancaster, Pennsylvania, in June 1995, entitled, "The Quiet in the Land? Women of Anabaptist Traditions in Historical Perspective." There were 256 participants from Canada, Germany, the Netherlands, and the United States. Papers presented examined women's experiences in Anabaptist traditions from the sixteenth through the twentieth centuries. Both academic and theological conferences such as these, focusing specifically on Mennonite women's experience, allows Mennonite women to discuss issues themselves in a way that, until recently, was not available to them.

These recent attempts for dialogue about women's theology and history have not seemed to cause the church leadership concern about women's role in the church, however, one particular conference has been upsetting, both to Mennonite leadership and to Mennonite women. In May of 1995, MCC B.C. had agreed to host an inter-Mennonite women's conference, one of a series of inter-Mennonite women's conferences which have been held in North America since 1975. One of the foci was to "support and encourage women to pursue their gifts at home, church and in their communities."[12] A month before the conference was held, MCC B.C. withdrew their support because of concerns from local MB and CMC church leaders who "raised questions about the theological views of one of the conference's keynote speakers."[13] A member of the planning committee felt that "some church leaders leapt to the conclusion that it [the conference] is radical feminist and New Age without ever getting adequate information."[14] Apparently, letters had been sent to MCC B.C., calling the conference a 'radical feminist' event. In spite of this, the conference proceeded, albeit without the support of MCC B.C. After the event, there were several articles and letters in the *Mennonite Reporter* about the conference. An MB pastor saw the women's conference "as a challenge to 'the decision made by the Mennonite Brethren of North America two years ago about women in ministry [not to allow women to be senior pastors].' "[15] One letter to the editor referred to the conference in connection with the "women in ministry debate."[16] Two years prior, the General Conference of MB churches had discussed women's ministry role at its annual conference. In preparation for the discussion, the book, *Your Daughters Shall Prophesy*, was published to serve as a catalyst for discussion.[17] It contained chapters by several MB scholars, some opposed to, and some in favor of, female pastoral leadership. At the Conference, a resolution was presented that would have allowed for "diversity of conviction and practice in the appointment of women to pastoral leadership in ways that are consistent with the governance patterns of the local congregation." When it was defeated, MB women in Manitoba organized an "MB Women's Network"[18] and produced a "Statement of Concern," signed by approximately 350 women and men, which expressed their concern

> that the Mennonite Brethren General Conference restriction of women
> in pastoral leadership misrepresents the Scriptural vision of gender

> equality. The July 1993 Conference decision to uphold this restriction
> perpetuates inequality, discourages many women from developing their
> gifts, and limits the effectiveness of the church in the world today.[19]

The mission of the Network was to promote "the full exercise of women's gifts in the life of the church."[20]   Recently, it sponsored a two-day conference promoting education and awareness of the issues.[21]

Since its founding, there has been some interchange between The Network and Mennonite women's societies. The MB Women's Network was invited to present workshops on women's leadership gifts and inclusive language at the Manitoba MB Women's Conference (a conference organized by members of women's societies in April 1994).   There were mixed reactions among participants. While some members in women's societies supported the initiatives of the MB Women's Network, others disapproved.

With the discontinuation of several Mennonite women's groups, and the increase in opportunities for Mennonite women to be involved in other initiatives, we wonder what makes Mennonite women's societies viable today. In the recent workshop alluded to earlier, "Demise or Rebirth," women

> gave a resounding NO to the possibility of demise. . . . All participants
> felt WM groups were very important in their lives, and had served as
> a tremendous support for the congregation in fellowshipping with each
> other, in visiting members of the church, and in carrying out various
> other important tasks.[22]

Many Mennonite women still feel there is much to be gained in the context of their gendered societies. In fact, in one church, a women's group that disbanded in the mid 1980s is considering reorganization.[23] While they wouldn't want to serve the local church in the same way as they did before the women's group discontinued, i.e., being responsible to prepare and serve church dinners, they expressed a need to meet for support and connection. They miss the friendship the group offered, the comfort in times of grief, and the companionship in time of loneliness. One woman stated that she believes there is a way in which women relate to each other that can not be achieved in a mixed group of women and men. Because of this, she feels that small church groups with female and male participants cannot take the place of women's societies. "I need my women friends," she said.[24]

This is a time of change and ferment; it is welcomed by some Mennonite women, resisted by others. When the older members of Mennonite women's societies will no longer be able to attend meetings, it is difficult to predict what the future will hold for women in Mennonite women's societies who gave so much to the church through the work of their hands.

Notes

1 Marlene Kruger Wiebe, "Change for women's groups include integration," *Mennonite Reporter* 25, 10 (15 May 1995): 15.

2 Lois Siemens, "Skits performed at women's conference," *Mennonite Reporter* 25, 12 (12 June 1995): 11.

3 Ingrid Janzen Lamp, "Women challenged to 'love the unlovely,' " *Mennonite Reporter* 25, 9 (1 May 1995): 14, and Gerta Funk and Connie Klassen, "Manitoba Women in Mission conference," *Mennonite Reporter* 25, 13 (26 June 1995): 14.

4 Katie Weinberger, "Women's groups join to hear Zaire mission worker," *Mennonite Reporter* 22, 22 (16 November 1992): 15.

5 Sarah Stoesz, "Demise or Rebirth," *CMC Nexus* 2, 1 (September 1995): 14. *CMC Nexus*, a periodical of the CMC, publishes nine times a year, seeking to link CMC congregations with each other and with the Conference offices.

6 Roma Quapp, "Bethel Women in Mission celebrate 50 years," *Mennonite Reporter* 25, 12 (12 June 1995): 11.

7 Lamp, "Women challenged to 'love the unlovely,' " p. 14.

8 Neufeld, ed., *History of Alberta Mennonite Women in Mission*, p. 10; and Helen Brown, "Alberta Women in Mission hear Bolivian missionary," *Mennonite Reporter* 21, 11 (27 May 1991): 10.

9 Irene Klassen, "Alberta women's groups ponder their future," *Mennonite Reporter* 25, 12 (12 June 1995): 11.

10 Stoesz, "Demise or Rebirth," p. 14.

11 Brochure advertising the conference, "In a Mennonite Voice: Women Doing Theology," 30 April - 2 May 1992, Conrad Grebel College, Waterloo, Ontario.

12 John Longhurst, "MCC B.C. withdraws support for women's conference over liturgy controversy," *Mennonite Reporter* 25, 11 (29 May 1995): B2.

13 Ibid., p. B1.

14 Ibid.

15 Ibid., p. B2.

16 George H. Epp, "Why does Coggins speak for others?" *Mennonite Reporter* 25, 19 (2 October 1995): 6.

17 Toews et al., *Your Daughters Shall Prophesy*.

18 Information on the background, mission, objectives, and initiatives of the MB Women's Network was obtained from Dale Taylor, member of the Steering Committee of the MB Women's Network.

19 "A Statement of Concern," MB Women's Network, 1993.

20 A segment of the mission statement of the MB Women's Network.

21 Wilma Derksen, "Women's network resumes dialogue at conference," *Mennonite Reporter* 25, 5 (6 March 1995): 1.

22 Stoesz, "Demise or Rebirth," p. 14.

23 Interview with Helene Dick, Elsa Koop, and Anni Wiebe, former members of the women's group in Ottawa Mennonite Church, Ottawa, Ontario, 22 October 1995.

24 Stated by Helene Dick in interview.

Appendix A

SURVEY ON WOMEN'S FELLOWSHIP GROUPS
OF THE CONFERENCE OF MENNONITES IN CANADA
AND THE CANADIAN MENNONITE BRETHREN

Name and address of person(s) who completed the survey

_____

_____

_____

1. Give the name of your church_____

2. PRESENT: Give the full name of your women's association

_____

PAST: If there have been changes in the name of your group, list the various changes and the years the changes were made.

_____

_____

3. What year did your group begin? _____

4. PRESENT: How often do you meet? _____ weekly _____ every second
week

_____ monthly _____ other

Does your group meet in the summer? _____Yes _____No

PAST: If the frequency of meeting has changed from past years, state the changes in frequency of meeting and the years the changes were made.

_____

5. PRESENT: In which languages(s) do you conduct your meetings?

    _____English   _____German   _____Other

    PAST: If your group used to use the German language and now has
    changed to English, when was that change made?_____

6. PRESENT: What is the purpose of your group? Mark them in the order
    of importance: 1, 2, 3, etc.

    _____ fellowship, friendship and support   _____ evangelize

    _____ to be of service to the local church   _____ missions

    _____ discuss contemporary issues of particular interest to women.

    (Name them)_____

    PAST: If the purpose of your group has changed from past years, list the
    changes in purpose and years in which they occurred.

    _____

    _____

7. PRESENT: What are you doing at your meetings this year? Mark as many
    as you need to.

    a. _____ Scripture reading   f. _____ study of other religious books

    b. _____ prayer   g. _____ have an offering

    c. _____ singing   h. _____ eat

    d. _____ Bible studies   i. _____ crafts

    e. _____ devotional   j. _____ discuss issues of importance
                                                 to the group

    _____ other (name them) _____

Which 3 of the above are most important in your group? (a,b,c, etc.)

_____

PAST: If there have been changes in what you do at your meetings, state the changes and the years in which they occurred.

_____

_____

8. PRESENT: What projects is your group supporting this year?

a. _____ raise money for foreign missions projects

b. _____ visit nursing homes in the community

c. _____ participate in World Day of Prayer

d. _____ work in MCC Self Help Stores

e. _____ raise money for MCC

f. _____ raise money for home missions projects

g. _____ supply furnishings for the local church like curtains, piano, dishes, floral arrangements, cribs

_____ other (name them) _____

Which 3 of the above projects are most important to your group?

_____

PAST: If there have been changes in the kind of projects your groups supports, list the changes and the years in which they occurred.

_____

_____

9. PRESENT: If your group raises money for various projects, what methods
    are being used this year?

    a. _____ church dinners   e. _____ bake sales

    b. _____ auctions   f. _____ fashion shows

    c. _____ bazaars (crafts sales)   g._____ garage sales

    d. _____ donations

    _____ other (name them)_____

    Which of the above methods are most important in raising money? (a,b,c,
    etc.)

    _____

    PAST: If this is a change from how money used to be raised, state former
    methods and the years in which they were practised.

    _____

10. If your group has a biblical motto, what is it?

    _____

11. Which Biblical texts have had an important impact on the development
    of your group's

    a. purpose   _____

    b. projects   _____

12. Approximately what percentage of women in your congregation belong to
    your group?

    _____75%-100% _____50%-74% _____25%-49% _____less than 25%

13. Approximately how many women between the following ages are:

	Part of your women's group	In your group and working outside the home
Ages		
20-30	_____	_____
31-40	_____	_____
41-50	_____	_____
51-60	_____	_____
61-70	_____	_____
71 +	_____	_____

14. If possible, consult your records and give the approximate average attendance for the following particular years:

1920 _____   1960 _____

1930 _____   1970 _____

1940 _____   1980 _____

1950 _____   1988 _____

15. Has participation in any of the following activities by women in your church affected attendance in your women's group? If so, which ones and how?

Church-sponsored Bible studies _____

Neighbourhood Bible studies_____

Church-sponsored mother's clubs _____

Church fellowship groups _____

Activities for personal development such as swimming, aerobics, night school classes_____

Other _____

16. If you are aware of any women's group in your church that has
    discontinued meeting, when did this occur and why?

    _____

    _____

17. If you wish to receive a summary of survey results, please check here [ ]

PLEASE REPLY BY JANUARY 15, 1989.

COVER LETTER

5 Beddoe Lane
Gloucester, Ont.
K1B 3X9
Nov. 4, 1988

Dear

Please give this letter to the president of one of the women's fellowship groups in your church. If your church does not have a women's group, I would very much appreciate your assistance by answering only questions 1 and 16 of the survey form and sending it back to me in the enclosed self-addressed stamped envelope.

I am presently working on a doctoral thesis on "An Examination of the Women's Fellowship Groups (auxiliaries, societies, Verein) of the General Conference and Mennonite Brethren Churches in Canada." I am limiting the study to those churches which were formed between 1895 and 1950. To my knowledge, the only research done in this area was by the provincial and national Women in Mission of the Conference of Mennonites in Canada in 1977. Therefore, in order to tell the story of Mennonite women's associations your participation is crucial. My hope is that my research can become the basis for a book on the history of Mennonite women's fellowship groups.

My interest in writing the history of the women's groups began last year when, for one of my classes at the University of Ottawa, I studied women's groups in 2 General Conference and 2 Mennonite Brethren churches in each of 5 provinces, examining minutes, reports, church histories and constitutions.

The story of the work of Canadian Mennonite women's groups is an important one. Women have been active in these groups since Mennonites first immigrated to Canada. They have found these groups to be a tremendous support to them personally, and as well, have raised substantial amounts of money in support of a variety of worthwhile projects.

To tell you a little bit about myself--I was raised in the Mennonite Brethren Church in Saskatoon, Sask. My husband, Vern, and I attended the Mennonite Brethren Biblical Seminary in Fresno, California and co-pastored the Mennonite Church in Thompson, Manitoba for three years. We have lived in Ottawa with our 3 children since 1985 and are presently members of the Ottawa Mennonite Church.

I am aware that in some churches there are more than one women's fellowship group. I would like one person from each group to fill out a survey. Please share this letter and give survey forms to the president (or other knowledgeable member) of each
women's group in your church. You may photocopy the survey form if I have not sent enough of them.

I am aware that many women's groups report to the church at the church's annual business meeting. I would very much appreciate a copy of these annual reports from each women's group in your church, plus the financial statement of each group for the following years: 1920, 30, 40, 50, 60, 70, 80, 88. As well, if the group has a constitution, or if there is additional information, documents or anecdotes which you think could be helpful I would appreciate receiving them. Send completed surveys and any other documents using the enclosed self-addressed stamped envelope to:
(additional postage is needed if more than 6 pages are enclosed)

Gloria Redekop
5 Beddoe Lane
Gloucester, Ontario
K1B 3X9

If you have any questions feel free to write or call me at 613-837-4218.

Thank you for your interest and cooperation in the writing of this important history of the women's fellowship groups of the Conference of Mennonites in Canada and the Canadian Mennonite Brethren.

Sincerely yours in Christian love,

_____

Gloria Redekop

Appendix B

Mennonite Women's Societies That Completed the Survey

Altona Willing Helpers (Altona Bergthaler Mennonite)
Arnaud Christian Fellowship (Arnaud Mennonite)
Benevolent Group (Greendale First Mennonite)
Bergthal Sewing Circle (Bergthal Mennonite)
Bergthaler Bethel Ladies Aid (Bergthaler Mennonite Church of Morden)
Bergthaler Ladies Aid (Morden Bergthaler Mennonite)
Bergthaler Ladies Fellowship (Winkler Bergthaler Mennonite)
Bethany Mennonite Ladies Aid (Bethany Mennonite)
Bethel Ladies Aid (Winkler Bergthaler Mennonite)
Bethel Women in Mission (Bethel Mennonite)
Bethesda Ladies Fellowship (Winkler Bergthaler Mennonite)
Blaine Lake Gospel Chapel unnamed women's group
Bridgeway Women's Fellowship (Bridgeway Community)
Broadway Women's Fellowship (Broadway MB)
Central Ladies Fellowship (Winnipeg Central MB)
Chapel Ladies Fellowship Group (Christian Fellowship Chapel in Orillia)
Cheerful Mission Circle (North Star Mennonite)
Concordia Ladies Aid (Rosemary Mennonite)
Countess Ladies Aid (Rosemary Mennonite)
Crystal City Mennonite Ladies Aid (Crystal City Mennonite)
Dorcas Fellowship Ladies Meetings (Willow Park MB)
Dorcas Ladies Circle (Clearbrook MB)
Dorcas Ruth (Yarrow MB)
Dunnville Women in Mission (Dunnville United Mennonite)
Ebenezer *Verein* (Steinbach Mennonite)
Edelweiss Circle (First Mennonite in Winnipeg)
Eden Ladies Fellowship (Eden Mennonite)
Eigenheim Mission Society (Eigenheim Mennonite)
Eigenheim Women's Fellowship (Eigenheim Mennonite)
Erie View Mission Circle (Erie View United Mennonite)
Evergreen Circle (First Mennonite in Winnipeg)
Eyebrow Mennonite Ladies Aid (Eyebrow Mennonite)
Feminine Focus (Central MB)
First Ladies Aid (Zoar Mennonite)
First Mennonite Mission Aid (Interdenominational group in Gretna)
First Senior Ladies Organization (First Mennonite in Winnipeg)
North Kildonan MB *Frauendienst*
Foothills Community Church Ladies Fellowship
Frauenverein (North Kildonan MB)

Frauenverein (Sargent Avenue Mennonite)
Freundinnenverein (First Mennonite in Winnipeg)
Friendly Hour (First Mennonite in Saskatoon)
Friendship Builders (Coaldale MB)
Friendship Circle (Clearbrook MB)
Friendship Circle of the Morden MB Church
Friendship Circle (Vineland United Mennonite)
Gem MB Ladies Fellowship
Glenbush Ladies Aid (Hoffnungsfelder Mennonite)
Glenbush MB Ladies Aid (Glenbush MB)
Glenlea Ladies Fellowship (Glenlea Mennonite)
Good Samaritan Club (Rosthern Mennonite)
Goodwill Club (Coaldale Mennonite)
Goodwill Fellowship Circle (Vauxhall MB)
Goodwill Ladies Aid (Rosthern Mennonite)
Goodwill Society (North Star Mennonite)
Grace Fellowship (Yarrow MB)
Grace Ladies Aid (Greendale MB)
Gretna Willing Helpers Ladies Aid (Gretna Bergthaler Mennonite)
Harmony Hearts (United Mennonite in Black Creek)
Helfer Verein (Vancouver MB)
Helping Hands of Arnold Community Church
Helping Hands Ladies Aid (Herschel Ebenfeld Mennonite)
Helping Hands Sewing Circle (Vineland United Mennonite)
Herbert MB Senior Ladies Aid
Herbert Mennonite Ladies Aid (Herbert Mennonite)
Hillside Christian Fellowship Church Women's Ministries
Homemakers Fellowship (Altona Bergthaler Mennonite)
Homemakers Fellowship (Dalmeny Community)
Homemakers Fellowship (Langham Zoar Mennonite)
Hope Mennonite Women in Mission
Justice Ladies Fellowship (Justice MB)
Kelstern Ladies Fellowship (Elim MB)
Kleeblatt Verein (First Mennonite in Winnipeg)
Koinonia (North Star Mennonite)
Koinonia Fellowship of the Portage Avenue MB Church
Koinonia Ladies Group (Altona Bergthaler Mennonite)
Ladies Aid (Hoffnungsfelder Mennonite)
Ladies Aid *Einigkeit* (First Mennonite in Calgary)
Ladies Bible Study Group (South Abbotsford MB)
Ladies Bible Study Fellowship (Harrison Gospel Chapel)
Ladies Christian Fellowship (Morden MB)
Ladies Christian Fellowship Group (Scott Street MB)

Ladies Fellowship (Borden MB)
Ladies Fellowship (Cedar Hills Mennonite)
Ladies Fellowship (Community Fellowship in Newton)
Ladies Fellowship (Elmwood MB)
Ladies Fellowship (Gospel Fellowship)
Ladies Fellowship (Lakeview MB)
Ladies Fellowship (Lowe Farm Bergthaler Mennonite)
Ladies Fellowship (Steinbach MB)
Ladies Fellowship Circle (Coaldale MB)
Ladies Fellowship Circle (Main Centre MB)
Ladies Friendship Circle (Port Rowan MB)
Ladies Friendship Hour (Scott Street MB)
Ladies Mission Circle (Woodrow Gospel Chapel)
Ladies Missionary Fellowship (Leamington MB)
Laird Fellowship Group (Laird Mennonite)
Laird Senior Ladies Aid (Laird Mennonite)
Lichtenauer Ladies Aide (Lichtenauer Mennonite)
Love and Light Ladies (Neuenlage Grace Mennonite)
Loving Deeds Ladies Group (Greendale First Mennonite)
Lucky Lake Christian Fellowship Ladies (Lucky Lake Christian Fellowship)
MacGregor Bergthaler Ladies Mission Group
Magdalene Ladies Aid (Hanley Mennonite)
Manitou Ladies Fellowship (Manitou MB)
Maranatha Ladies Fellowship (Clearbrook MB)
Maria Martha Verein (Clearbrook Mennonite)
Maria Martha Verein (Elim Mennonite)
Maria-Martha Verein (Clearbrook MB)
Marisa Mission Group (Plum Coulee Bergthaler Mennonite)
Mary-Martha Fellowship (South Abbotsford MB)
Mary Martha Group (Greendale First Mennonite)
Mary Martha Mission Group (Altona Bergthaler Mennonite)
MB Ladies Fellowship (Herbert MB)
Mission Circle (Waterloo-Kitchener United Mennonite)
Mission Mennonite Sewing Circle (Cedar Valley Mennonite)
Missionary Fellowship Group (Elm Creek MB)
Missionary Prayer Band (Central MB)
Missionettes (Bethel Mennonite)
Missions Group (Lakeview MB)
Missions Sewing Circle (Steinbach Mennonite)
Missions Verein (Coaldale MB)
Missionsverein (Bergthaler Mennonite of Morden)
Morija Woman's Circle (First Mennonite)
MYWA (Tofield Mennonite)

Naomi Mission Society (First Mennonite in Saskatoon)
Naomi Ruth Verein (First United Mennonite in Vancouver)
Niagara United Mennonite Ladies Aid #3 (Niagara United Mennonite)
Niagara United Mennonite Ladies Aid #2 (Niagara United Mennonite)
Niverville Mennonite Church Mission Sisters (Niverville Mennonite)
Oak Lake Mennonite Ladies Aid (Oak Lake Mennonite)
Open Door Fellowship (Central Heights MB)
Parliament Community Ladies Fellowship
Pigeon Lake Ladies Aid (Schoenfelder Mennonite)
Pleasant Hour (Broadway MB)
Pleasant Point Ladies Aid (Pleasant Point Mennonite)
Rabbit Lake Mennonite Ladies Aid (Hoffnungsfelder Mennonite)
REAH (South Langley MB)
Rosenfeld Ladies Fellowship (Rosenfeld Bergthaler Mennonite)
Rosentaler Verein (First Mennonite)
Rosthern Willing Helpers Ladies Aid
Salome Verein (Yarrow MB)
Sargent Avenue *Missionsverein*
Schwestern Verein (Niverville MB)
Schwester Verein of the Winkler MB Church
Senior Ladies Aid (Carrot River Mennonite)
Senior Ladies Aid (First Mennonite)
Senior Ladies Group (Portage Avenue MB)
Senior Ladies Mission Society (Cornerstone Mennonite)
Senior Women's Fellowship (Central MB)
Servettes (Waterloo-Kitchener United Mennonite)
Sonnenstrahl Verein (First Mennonite in Kelowna)
South Abbotsford Ladies Fellowship (South Abbotsford MB)
South Western Ontario Women in Mission (Leamington United Mennonite)
Springridge Church Women (Springridge Mennonite)
Sunbeam Ladies Aid (Steinbach Mennonite)
Sunbeam Mission Band (Coaldale MB)
Sunbeam Sewing Circle (Coaldale Mennonite)
Tabea Sewing Circle (Altona Bergthaler Commerfelder EMMC)
Tabea Verein (Clearbrook MB)
The Willing Workers (Springstein Mennonite)
Tiefengrund Senior Ladies Aid (Tiefengrund Rosenort Mennonite)
Tiefengrund Women in Mission (Tiefengrund Rosenort Mennonite)
Verein #13 (Leamington United Mennonite)
Verein #19 (Leamington United Mennonite)
Warman MB Ladies Fellowship
Westview Community Ladies Group (Westview Community Church)
Willing Hands (Cedar Hills Mennonite)

Willing Hands Ladies Aid (Yarrow United Mennonite)
Willing Helpers Club (Elmwood MB)
Willing Helpers Ladies Aid (Rosemary Mennonite)
Wingham Mennonite Ladies Aid (Wingham Mennonite)
Wohltätigkeits Verein-Benevolent Society (First United Mennonite in
    Vancouver)
Women in Mission of the Homewood Mennonite Church
Women in Missions Fellowship (Nordheim Mennonite)
Women's Auxiliary of the Fiske Mennonite Church (Fiske Mennonite)
Women's Christian Fellowship (Grace Mennonite)
Women's Christian Fellowship (Linden MB)
Women's Christian Fellowship (Rosemary Mennonite)
Women's Christian's Endeavour Group (Vineland United Mennonite)
Women's Fellowship (Sargent Avenue Mennonite)
Women's Mission Circle (Philadelphia MB)
Women's Missionary Association (Stirling Avenue Mennonite)
Women's Missionary Fellowship of the Arelee MB Church
Women's Missionary Service (Hepburn MB)
Women's Service and Fellowship (Niverville MB)
Wymark Ladies Mission Club (Emmaus Mennonite)
Young Ladies Fellowship (Vancouver MB)
Young Women's Fellowship (Bergthal Mennonite)
Zion Mennonite Senior Ladies Aid

Bibliography

1. Primary Sources

Minutes and Annual Reports of Mennonite Women's Societies

Women's Societies of the Conference of Mennonites in Canada

Arnaud, Manitoba. Report. Margaret Kathler, "Arnaud Christian Fellowship," 1984.

Black Creek, British Columbia. United Mennonite Church. Minutes. Gay Wedel, "Harmony Hearts Report–1980," 1980.

Canadian Women in Mission. Canadian Women in Mission 30th Conference. Report. Anna Ens, "Leadership: Christ our Model," 3 July 1982.

Canadian Women in Mission. Minutes. "Minutes of the 21st Canadian Women's Conference," 7 July 1973.

Canadian Women in Mission. Report. Margaret Ewert, "President's Report to the Canadian Women in Mission 26th Annual Conference," 7 July 1978.

Canadian Women in Mission. Report. Anita Froese, President, Canadian Women in Mission, "From Anita's Desk (Report–1985)," 1985.

Canadian Women in Mission. Report. Anita Froese, President, Canadian Women in Mission, "Reflections," 1987.

Canadian Women in Mission. "Women's Conference Themes," 1953-78.

Carrot River, Saskatchewan. Mennonite Senior Ladies Aid. "Financial Report," 1988.

Council of Boards of the Conference of Mennonites in Canada. Minutes. Anita Froese, President, Canadian Women in Mission President, "Opening Devotional–Council of Boards," 28 January 1982.

Drake, Saskatchewan. North Star Mennonite Church. Report. "North Star Senior Ladies Aid," n.d.

Hanley, Saskatchewan. Hanley Mennonite Church. Minutes. Helen Froese, "Report of the Magdalene Ladies Aid for 1980."

Niverville, Manitoba. Niverville Mennonite Church. Minutes. Helen Friesen, "Mission Sisters' Report," 1980, and Mary Anne Reimer, "Mission Sisters' Report," 1988.

Oaklake, Manitoba. Oaklake Mennonite Church. Minutes. Rosie Sawatsky, "Ladies Aid Activities," 1971.

Rosemary, Alberta. Rosemary Mennonite Church. Minutes. "Concordia Ladies Aid for 1988."

Saskatoon, Saskatchewan. Friendly Hour Club. First Mennonite Church. Annual Report, 1961.

Winnipeg, Manitoba. Sargent Avenue Mennonite Church. Minutes. Tina Friesen, "*Missionsverein*," 1979-80.

Women's Societies of the Canadian Mennonite Brethren

Dalmeny, Saskatchewan. Dalmeny Community Church. Minutes. Margaret
    Lepp, "Homemaker's Report," 1980. Herbert, Saskatchewan.
Herbert Mennonite Brethren Church. Minutes. Tina Block, "Junior Ladies Aid
    Report," 1977, p. 20; 1976, p. 5.
Main Centre, Saskatchewan. Main Centre Mennonite Brethren Church. Minutes.
    "Ladies Aid Report," 1979, and Diane Unruh, "Ladies Aid Report,"
    1982.
Newton, Manitoba. Community Fellowship Mennonite Brethren Church.
    Minutes. Grace Loewen, "Ladies Fellowship Report," 1988.
Regina, Saskatchewan. Ladies Fellowship of the Parliament Mennonite Brethren
    Church. Report. Betty Russell, "Ladies Fellowship," 1988.
Saskatoon, Saskatchewan. Central Mennonite Brethren Church. Minutes.
    Albertine Speiser, "Missionary Prayer Band," 1978; Donna Smith,
    "Women Alive Report," 1979; Elizabeth Andres, "Senior Women's
    Fellowship," 1982; Elizabeth Wall, "Missionary Prayer Band," 1983.
South Saskatchewan Mennonite Brethren Ladies Auxiliary. Minutes. 1959-87.
Women's Conference of the Manitoba Mennonite Brethren Churches. Minutes.
    "Minutes of the Eighth Annual Women's Conference of the Manitoba
    Mennonite Brethren Churches," 1974.
Women's Conference of the Manitoba Mennonite Brethren Churches. Report.
    "Report of the Women's Conference of the Manitoba Mennonite
    Brethren Churches," 17 June 1967.
Women's Conference of the Manitoba Mennonite Brethren Churches. Report.
    "Spring Conference–April 21, 1979."
Women's Conference of the Manitoba Mennonite Brethren Churches. Report.
    Tina Brown, "President's Report 1973."

Constitutions

Women's Societies of the Conference of Mennonites in Canada

Canadian Women in Mission. "Constitution of Canadian Women in Mission,"
    1953.
Magdalene Ladies Aid and Hanley Ladies Aid. Hanley Mennonite Church.
    Hanley, Saskatchewan. Lillian Patkau, Tena Patkau, Irene Froese, Helen
    Froese, and Justine Schellenberg, "Constitution," 1982.
Naomi Mission Society. First Mennonite Church. Saskatoon, Saskatchewan,
    1975.

Women's Societies of the Canadian Mennonite Brethren

Manitou Mennonite Brethren Ladies Fellowship. Manitou Mennonite Brethren Church. Manitou, Manitoba. 1981.

Southern Saskatchewan Mennonite Ladies Fellowship. Revised Constitution. "Constitution of the Southern Saskatchewan Mennonite Brethren Ladies Fellowship," Spring Meeting 1988.

Women's Conference of the Mennonite Brethren Church of Manitoba. "Constitution of the Women's Conference of the Mennonite Brethren Church of Manitoba," 1980.

Women's Mennonite Brethren Missionary Auxiliary of South Saskatchewan. "Constitution of the Women's Mennonite Brethren Missionary Auxiliary of South Saskatchewan," 1964.

Interviews

Craig, Daphne. Interview with author. Gloucester, Ontario, 1988.

Dick, Helene, Elsa Koop, and Annie Wiebe. Former members of the women's group in Ottawa Mennonite Church. Interview with author. Ottawa, Ontario, 22 October 1995.

Kornelsen, Heidi. Interview with author. Edmonton, Alberta, August 1969.

Langeman, Katharine, Helen Peters, Hedie Wiens, Margaret Wiens, and Anna Fast. George Street Senior Home of the Waterloo/Kitchener United Mennonite Church. Interviews with author. Waterloo, Ontario, 19 March 1989.

Redekopp, Antonio, and Benjamin Redekopp of St. Catharines, Ontario. Interview with author. Ottawa, Ontario, 24 May 1989.

Sampson, Joan. Interview with author. Ottawa, Ontario, 1988.

Letters and Poems

Heinrichs, Verna. Letter to author. Manitou, Manitoba, 1988.

Janzen, Heinz. *Gedicht* [Poem], a poem on donations by Mennonite women's societies of the Waterloo/Kitchener Mennonite Church to replace the church roof. Waterloo, Ontario, late 1940s.

Klassen, Catherine. Letter to author. Winnipeg, Manitoba, 25 April 1989.

Pleasant Point Ladies Aid. Letter to author. Clavet, Saskatchewan, 1988.

Regehr, Mrs. W. Letter to Board of Missions and Services, "Women's Conference of the Manitoba Mennonite Brethren Churches Minutes and Correspondence," 1967-69.

Wiebe, Katie Funk. Letter to the leaders of women's organizations in General Conference churches, 1977.

Local Church Histories

Conference of Mennonites in Canada

Albrecht, Henry, G.G. Neufeld, Jake J. Heide, Jake Unger, and Peter Neufeld. *History of the Whitewater Mennonite Church Boissevain, Manitoba 1927-1987*. Boissevain: Whitewater Mennonite Church, 1987.

Bethel Mennonite Church (1936-1980), Aldergrove, B.C.. Altona: D.W. Friesen and Sons, 1980.

Driedger, N.N. *The Leamington United Mennonite Church: Establishment and Development 1925-1972*. Altona: D.W. Friesen and Sons, 1972.

Dyck, Gert. "Wymark Ladies Mission Club." In *Patchwork of Memories*. N.p., n.d.

Friesen, Helena. "The Hochfeld Sewing Circle." In *A History of the Hague Mennonite Church, Hague Saskatchewan 1900-1975*. Edited by John D.Rempel. Rosthern: Hague Mennonite Church, 1975.

John Giesbrecht, George Dyck, Rev. N.N. Fransen, Mary Klassen-Neudorf, and Lydia Wichert. *Highlights of the Vineland United Mennonite Church (1936-1986)*. N.p., 1986.

A History of the First Mennonite Church, Greendale B.C. Greendale: First Mennonite Church, 1976.

Klassen, H.T. *Birth and Growth of the Eigenheim Mennonite Church 1892-1974*. Rosthern: Eigenheim Mennonite Church, 1974.

Mennonite Church Rosemary. Altona: D.W. Friesen and Sons, 1980.

The Niagara United Mennonite Church 1938-1988. Niagara: Niagara United Mennonite Church, 1988.

Patkau, Esther, ed. *First Mennonite Church in Saskatoon, 1923-1982*. Saskatoon: First Mennonite Church, 1982.

_____. *Nordheimer Mennonite Church of Saskatchewan (1925-1975)*. Hanley: Nordheimer Mennonite Church, 1975.

Rempel, John D., ed. *A History of the Hague Mennonite Church, Hague Saskatchewan 1900-1975*. Rosthern: Hague Mennonite Church, 1975.

Thiessen, Katharina. "Later Development of the Ladies' Circle." In *A History of the First Mennonite Church, Greendale B.C.* Greendale: First Mennonite Church, 1976.

Canadian Mennonite Brethren

"Arelee MB Missionary Fellowship." *Arelee and District History*. N.p., 1982.

Boldt, Edward, ed. *A History of the Ontario Conference of Mennonite Brethren Churches 1957-1982*. N.p., 1982.

Enns, Louise. "Ladies fellowship groups, Clearbrook MB Church." *History of the Clearbrook MB Church: 1936-1986*. N.p., 1986.

Harder, Katherine, ed. *The Greendale Mennonite Brethren Church (1931-1981)*. Cloverdale: Greendale Mennonite Brethren Church, 1981.

History of the Clearbrook MB Church: 1936-1986. N.p., 1986.

Leamington Mennonite Brethren Church. N.p., n.d.

Mennonite Brethren Church Winkler, Manitoba (1888-1963). N.p., n.d.

Pauls, Mary. "The Arnaud Mennonite Brethren Ladies' Fellowship." In *Arnaud Through the Years*, pp. 75-77. Edited by Christine M. Nichols. Steinbach: Derksen Printers, 1974

Redekopp, Elly. "Ladies Sewing Circles." In *Virgil MB Church (1937-1987)*. Edited by Helen Reimer Bergman. N.p., 1987.

Rempel, Esther (Bergman). "Ladies Aid." In *Borden Mennonite Brethren Church: Precious Memories (1905-1980)*. Edited by Orla Block. N.p.: n.d.

Teigrob, David. *What Mean These Stones? Mennonite Brethren Church Port Rowan (1925-1977)*. St. Catharines: Knight Publishing and Lincoln Graphics, 1979.

Mennonite Yearbooks

Yearbooks of the Conference of Mennonites in Canada

"Bill C. An Act to Incorporate Conference of Mennonites in Canada." In *Konferenz* [Conference]. Coaldale: Conference of Mennonites in Canada, 1947.

"Canadian Women in Mission 34th Annual Conference." In *Yearbook: Conference of Mennonites in Canada*. Winnipeg: Conference of Mennonites in Canada, 1986.

Neufeld, Anne. "Canadian Women in Mission Minutes–27th Annual Conference." In *Yearbook: Conference of Mennonites in Canada*. Winnipeg: Conference of Mennonites in Canada, 1979.

Redekopp, Mrs. P. "Canadian Women's Missionary Conference–1967." In *Yearbook: Conference of Mennonites in Canada*. Winnipeg: Conference of Mennonites in Canada, 1967.

Yearbook: Conference of Mennonites in Canada. Winnipeg: Conference of Mennonites in Canada, 1974, 1979, 1980-83. 1986, and 1988.

Yearbooks of the Canadian Conference of the Mennonite Brethren Church

1952 Yearbook of the Forty-Second Canadian Conference of the Mennonite Brethren Church of North America. Winnipeg: Canadian Conference of Mennonite Brethren Churches, 1952.

1975 Yearbook of the Sixty-Fifth Canadian Conference of the Mennonite Brethren Church of North America. Winnipeg: Canadian Conference of

Mennonite Brethren Churches, 1975.

Yearbook of the Canadian Conference of Mennonite Brethren Churches.
Winnipeg: Canadian Conference of Mennonite Brethren Churches, 1988.

*Yearbooks of the General Conference of the Mennonite Brethren
Church of North America*

General Conference Yearbook. 1879.

*Yearbook of the Forty-Seventh General Conference of the Mennonite Brethren
Church of North America.* Hillsboro: Mennonite Brethren Publishing
House, 1957.

*Yearbook of the Forty-Sixth General Conference of the Mennonite Brethren
Church of North America.* Hillsboro: Mennonite Brethren Publishing
House, 1954.

Yearbook of the General Conference of Mennonite Brethren Churches.
Hillsboro: Mennonite Brethren Publishing House, 1981.

*Yearbooks of the Provincial Conference of the Mennonite Brethren
Churches in Ontario*

Enns, Olga G. "Women's Missionary Service." In *Yearbook of the Thirty-Fifth
Annual Provincial Conference of the Mennonite Brethren Churches in
Ontario.* N.p.: Conference of the Mennonite Brethren Churches of
Ontario, 1966.

Dueck, Mary. "Report." In *Yearbook of the Forty-First Annual Provincial
Conference of the Mennonite Brethren Churches in Ontario.* N.p.:
Conference of the Mennonite Brethren Churches of Ontario, 1972.

_____. "Women's Missionary Service of the Ontario Mennonite Brethren
Conference." In *Yearbook of the Fortieth Annual Provincial Conference
of the Mennonite Brethren Churches in Ontario.* N.p.: Conference of
the Mennonite Brethren Churches of Ontario, 1971.

Heide, Loretta. "Women's Missionary Service of the Ontario Mennonite
Brethren Conference." In *Yearbook of the Fifty-Third Annual Provincial
Conference of the Mennonite Brethren Churches in Ontario.* N.p.:
Conference of the Mennonite Brethren Churches of Ontario, 1984.

Suderman, Elva A. "Women's Missionary Service Report." In *Yearbook of the
Forty-Fifth Annual Provincial Conference of the Mennonite Brethren
Churches in Ontario.* N.p.: Conference of the Mennonite Brethren
Churches of Ontario, 1976

"Women's Conference: MB Churches of Manitoba." In *1967 Yearbook of the
Thirty-Third Annual Manitoba Conference of MB Churches.* Winnipeg:
Conference of MB Churches of Manitoba, 1967.

Articles in Church Periodicals

Periodicals of the Conference of Mennonites in Canada

Bargen, Anne. "Making a marriage last." *The Canadian Mennonite* 4 (28 September 1956): 4.

_____. "Too gifted to become a mere housewife?" *The Canadian Mennonite* 4 (7 September 1956) :2.

Brown, Helen. "Alberta Women in Mission hear Bolivian missionary." *Mennonite Reporter* 21, 11 (27 May 1991): 10.

Derksen, Wilma. "Women's network resumes dialogue at conference," *Mennonite Reporter* 25, 5 (6 March 1995): 1.

Dick, Helen. "A mother and her career child." *The Canadian Mennonite* 17 (26 September 1969): 11.

"Die Arbeit des Frauenverein der 'Ersten Mennonitengemeinde' in Winnipeg." *Der Bote* (8 Dezember 1959):1.

Dueck, Mary Regehr. "The role of women (2): In church 'people' means 'men'." *Mennonite Reporter* 3 (19 March 1973): 7.

_____. "The role of women (3): Young maidens dare not prophesy." *Mennonite Reporter* 3 (2 April 1973): 7.

Durksen, Hedy. "Is life passing you by?" *The Canadian Mennonite* 9 (3 February 1961): 1.

_____. "The ladies' class." *The Canadian Mennonite* 9 (23 June 1961): 7.

_____. "Where do we stand?" *The Canadian Mennonite* 10 (30 March 1962): 8.

Dyck, Marie. "Fleiszige Frauenhånde." *Der Bote* (30 November 1955): 32, 46.

Epp, George H. "Why does Coggins speak for others?" *Mennonite Reporter* 25,19 (2 October 1995): 6.

Funk, Gerta and Connie Klassen,. "Manitoba Women in Mission conference." *Mennonite Reporter* 25, 13 (26 June 1995): 14.

Funk, Mrs. Henry. "Women stress foreign missions and the home." *The Canadian Mennonite* 16 (13 August 1968): 14.

Hostetter, B. Charles. "The husband's part in happy home building." *The Canadian Mennonite* 2 (27 August 1954): 6.

_____. "The wife's part in happy home building." *The Canadian Mennonite* 2 (3 September 1954) :6.

Kehler, Larry. "Mere motherhood?" *The Canadian Mennonite* 9 (4 August 1961):2.

_____. "The secretary." *The Canadian Mennonite* 10 (23 March 1962): 2.

Kehler, Lydia. "Troubled about 'Women's lib' discussion." *Mennonite Reporter* 4, 3 (4 February 1974): 7.

Klassen, Irene. "Alberta women's groups ponder their future." *Mennonite Reporter* 25, 12 (12 June 1995): 11.

Klaassen, Ruth. "The role of women (1): Keeping up with our Anabaptist sisters." *Mennonite Reporter* 3 (5 February 1973): 7.

Lamp, Ingrid Janzen. "Women challenged to 'love the unlovely,' " *Mennonite Reporter* 25, 9 (1 May 1995): 14.

_____. "Women hear reports from at home and abroad." *Mennonite Reporter* 24, 9 (2 May 1994): 11.

Longhurst, John. "MCC B.C. withdraws support for women's conference over liturgy controversy." *Mennonite Reporter* 25, 11 (29 May 1995): B2.

Neufeld, Elsie. "Manitoba women met at Boissevain." *The Canadian Mennonite*. 11 (7 June 1963): 3.

"Newton pioneers work program for women." *The Canadian Mennonite* 5 (25 January 1957): 1.

"A new feature begins in this issue." *The Canadian Mennonite* 9 (3 February 1961): 1.

"On inclusiveness in our fellowship." *Mennonite Reporter* 17 (27 July 1987): 18.

Penner, Elaine. "Few church women aspire to 'male' jobs–at least not yet." *The Canadian Mennonite* 17 (9 May 1969): 5.

Peters, John F. "Christian feminism: A husband's perspective." *Mennonite Reporter* 6 (20 September 1976): 7.

"The place of women in church work today." *The Canadian Mennonite* 5 (18 October 1957): 1.

"Portrait of a Pioneer: Heinrich H. Hamm pioneered in civic and church affairs." *The Canadian Mennonite* 2 (20 August 1954): 4.

Quapp, Roma. "Bethel Women in Mission celebrate 50 years." *Mennonite Reporter* 25, 12 (12 June 1995): 11.

Rempel, Ron. "Florence Driedger appointed president of General Conference Mennonite Church." *Mennonite Reporter* 17 (30 March 1987): 1-2.

Schroeder, Anna L."In and out of my window." *The Canadian Mennonite* 13 (7 September 1965): 12

_____. "My husband won't let me." *The Canadian Mennonite* 14 (12 July 1966): 20.

Shelly, Patty. "The role of women (4): The language must be changed." *Mennonite Reporter* 4 (16 April 1973): 7.

Siemens, Lois. "Skits performed at women's conference." *Mennonite Reporter* 25, 12 (12 June 1995): 11.

"The single girl." *The Canadian Mennonite* 5 (4 October 1957): 2.

Stoesz, Sarah. "Demise or Rebirth." *CMC Nexus* 2, 1 (September 1995): 14.

Weinberger, Katie. "Women's groups join to hear Zaire mission worker." *Mennonite Reporter* 22, 22 (16 November 1992): 15.

"What's a good wife worth?" *The Canadian Mennonite* 13 (28 September 1965): 12.

"Why Christian married women work." *The Canadian Mennonite* 3 (21 January 1955): 7.

Wiebe, Katie Funk. "The feminine mystique (1)." *The Canadian Mennonite* 14 (29 March 1966): 52.

_____. "The feminine mystique (2)." *The Canadian Mennonite* 14 (5 April 1966): 10.

_____. "Mennonite Brethren Women: Images and Realities of the Early Years," *Mennonite Life*. 36, 3 (September 1981): 22.

_____. "The place of women in the work of the church." *The Canadian Mennonite* 11 (1 March 1963): 5.

Wiebe, Marlene Kruger. "Change for women's groups include integration." *Mennonite Reporter* 25, 10 (15 May 1995): 15.

Wiebe, Menno. "Women's Conference more than peripheral." *Mennonite Reporter* 2, 15b (24 July 1972): 4.

"Women in Church Vocations–A service and fellowship opportunity for girls." *The Canadian Mennonite* 6 (1 August 1958): 5.

Periodicals of the Canadian Mennonite Brethren Church

"*An die Frauenvereine!*" *Mennonitische Rundschau* (16 Januar 1935): 6.

Bartel, Rudy. "Somewhat Uneasy." *Mennonite Brethren Herald* 15, 10 (14 May 1976): 9.

Bergen, Shirley. "Not True to Life." *Mennonite Brethren Herald* 15, 9 (30 April 1976): 8-9.

Dyck, Mrs. Ernest. "Women's meeting in BC." *Mennonite Brethren Herald* 3, 19 (8 May 1964): 13.

_____. "BC Missionary Fellowship annual meeting." *Mennonite Brethren Herald* 3, 42 (23 October 1964): 6.

Ewert, David. "Women in the Church." *Mennonite Brethren Herald*. 5, 8 (25 February 1966): 6.

Fehr, Mary. "Husband and wife ministry." *Mennonite Brethren Herald* 27, 3 (5 February 1988): 2.

"*Frauenvereinsarbeit.*" *Mennonitische Rundschau* (7 März 1935): 5.

Froese, Hilda. "The Ministry of women in the Christian Church," Parts 1, 2, and 3. *Mennonite Brethren Herald* 3, 21 (22 May 1964): 13; 25 (19 June 1964): 13; and 27 (3 July 1964): 12.

Giesbrecht, Lillian. "What makes a ladies aid profitable?" *Mennonite Brethren Herald* 5, 22 (10 June 1966): 16-17.

Guenther, Allen R. and Herbert Swartz. "The Role of Women in the Church." *Mennonite Brethren Herald* 12, 9 (4 May 1973): 4-9.

Jantz, Neoma. "Ontario ladies meet for spring rally." *Mennonite Brethren Herald* 3, 17 (24 April 1964): 13.

Kopp, Herb, ed. "The Mennonite Brethren Church in Canada: A Century of Grace." *Mennonite Brethren Herald* 27, 11 (27 May 1988): 2-72.

Loewen, Dave. "Freedom through Submission." *Mennonite Brethren Herald*

115, 9 (30 April 1976): 8,9.

Loewen Howard. "The Pauline View of Woman." *Direction* VI (October 1977): 3-20.

Martens, Hedy L. "God's Word: To Women as to Men." *Direction* V, 1 (January 1976): 11-25.

Ratzlaff, Don. "General Conference Reports: Board of Reference and Counsel." *Mennonite Brethren Herald* 26, 16 (28 August 1987): 16.

Redekop, John H. "Sexist Language." *Mennonite Brethren Herald* 22, 22 (2 December 1983): 12.

_____. "Women–Second Class Christians." *Mennonite Brethren Herald* 5, 23 (24 June 1966): 2.

Redekopp, I.W. "The Woman's Place in the Church." *Mennonite Brethren Herald* 2, 11 (15 March 1963): 5.

Reimer, Luetta. "A Christian Response to the Women's Liberation Movement." *Direction* III, 1 (April 1974): 167-172.

Suderman, Jacob. "Christian Authority for Marriage and the Home." *Mennonite Brethren Herald*. 1, 36 (28 September 1962): 6-7.

Toews, John E. "The Role of Women in the Church: The Pauline Perspective." *Direction* IX, 1 (January 1980): 25-35.

Wiebe, Katie Funk. "Unfinished Business." *Mennonite Brethren Herald* 8, 26 (26 December 1969): 18-19.

_____. "The Women's Class." *Mennonite Brethren Herald*. 6, 1 (6 January 1967): 16.

_____. "Woman's Freedom–The Church's Necessity." *Direction* I, 3 (July 1972).

Wiens, Marie K. "Full Church Citizenship for Women?" *Mennonite Brethren Herald* 12 ,9 (4 May 1973): 18

Inter-Mennonite Periodicals

Bargen, Peter F. "The Coming of the Mennonites to Alberta." *Mennonite Life* 11, 2 (April 1956): 83-87.

Enns, J.H. "City with Largest Mennonite Population: Winnipeg, Manitoba." *Mennonite Life*. 11, 3 (July 1956): 112-114.

Janzen, Waldemar. "Foreign Mission Interest of the Mennonites in Russia Before World War I." *Mennonite Quarterly Review* 42, 1 (1968): 57-67.

Lohrenz, J.H. "The Mennonites in Winnipeg." *Mennonite Life* 6, 1 (January 1951): 16-25.

Mennonite Central Committee Peace Section Task Force on Women in Church and Society. *Report*. 18 (February 1978): 1-7.

Paetkau, Peter and Lawrence Klippenstein. "Conference of Mennonites in Canada: Background and Origin." *Mennonite Life* 34, 4 (December 1979): 4-10.

Wiebe, Joan. "Forum for leadership development." *Mennonite Central Committee Peace Section Task Force on Women in Church and Society Report* 18 (February 1978): 4.

Wiens, B.B. "Pioneering in British Columbia." *Mennonite Life* 1, 2 (July 1946): 9-13.

Wiens, Marie K. "No national organization." *Mennonite Central Committee Peace Section Task Force on Women in Church and Society Report* 18 (February 1978): 6.

Other Primary Sources

Banman, Jennifer. "Osler Mennonite Church," unpublished paper prepared for a Religious Studies course at Canadian Mennonite Bible College, Winnipeg, Manitoba, April 1982.

General Conference of Mennonite Brethren Churches. General Conference Study Conference Paper. David Ewert, "The Place of the Woman in the Church," May 1980.

Hershberger, Janice, ed. *Handbook of Information*. Newton: General Conference Mennonite Church, 1988.

Horsch, James E., ed. *Mennonite Yearbook and Directory*. Vol. 79. Scottdale: Mennonite Publishing House, 1990.

"In a Mennonite Voice: Women Doing Theology." Brochure to advertise the conference held at Conrad Grebel College, Waterloo, Ontario, 30 April - 2 May 1992.

MB Women's Network. Information on its initiatives obtained from Dale Taylor, member of the Steering Committee of the Network.

MB Women's Network. *A Statement of Concern*. 1993.

Regina, Saskatchewan. South Saskatchewan Mennonite Brethren Ladies Auxiliary. Bulletin. South Saskatchewan Mennonite Brethren Ladies Fall Auxiliary Meeting, 1 November 1986.

Report of the Royal Commission on the Status of Women. Ottawa: Information Canada, 1970.

Simons, Menno. "Comforting Letter to a Widow." In *The Complete Writings of Menno Simons*, pp. 1028-29. Edited by J.C. Wenger. Translated by Leonard Verduin. Scottdale: Herald Press, 1956.

_____. "Foundation of Christian Doctrine." In *The Complete Writings of Menno Simons*, pp. 105-226. Edited by J.C. Wenger. Translated by Leonard Verduin. Scottdale: Herald Press, 1956.

_____. "Sincere Appeal to Leonard Bouwen's Wife." In *The Complete Writings of Menno Simons*, pp. 1038-40. Edited by J.C. Wenger. Translated by Leonard Verduin. Scottdale: Herald Press, 1956.

_____. "The True Christian Faith." In *The Complete Writings of Menno Simons*, pp. 324-405. Edited by J.C. Wenger. Translated by Leonard

Verduin. Scottdale: Herald Press, 1956.

_____. "Why I do No Cease Teaching and Writing." In *The Complete Writings of Menno Simons*, pp. 305-307. Edited by J.C. Wenger. Translated by Leonard Verduin. Scottdale: Herald Press, 1956.

van Braght, Thieleman J. *Martyrs' Mirror of the Defenseless Christians*. Translated by Joseph F. Sohm. Lancaster County: N.p., 1837.

Wenger, J.C., ed. *The Complete Writings of Menno Simons*. Translated by Leonard Verduin. Scottdale: Herald Press, 1956.

2. Secondary Sources

Mennonite History

Bekker, Jacob P. *Origin of The Mennonite Brethren Church*. Translated by D.E. Pauls and A.E. Janzen. Hillsboro: Mennonite Brethren Historical Society of the Midwest, 1973.

Bender, Harold S., and C. Henry Smith, eds. *Mennonite Encyclopedia*. 4 vols. Scottdale: Mennonite Publishing House, 1955-57, 1959.

Board of Foreign Missions, *Missionary Album*. Hillsboro: Conference of the Mennonite Brethren Church, 1956.

Dyck, Cornelius J., ed. *An Introduction to Mennonite History*. Scottdale: Herald Press, 1967.

Epp, Frank H. *Mennonite Exodus: The Rescue and Resettlement of the Russian Mennonites Since the Communist Revolution*. Altona: D.W. Friesen and Sons, 1962.

_____. *Mennonites in Canada, 1786-1920: The History of a Separate People*. Toronto: Macmillan, 1974.

_____. *Mennonites in Canada, 1920-1940: A People's Struggle for Survival*. Toronto: Macmillan, 1982.

Esau, Mrs. H.T. *First Sixty Years of M.B. Missions*. Hillsboro: Mennonite Brethren Publishing House, 1954.

Friesen, Peter M. *The Mennonite Brotherhood in Russia (1789-1910)*. Edited and translated by J.B. Toews et al. Fresno: General Conference of Mennonite Brethren Churches, 1978.

Kauffman, J. Howard, and Leo Driedger. *The Mennonite Mosaic: Identity and Modernization*. Scottdale: Herald Press, 1991.

Klassen, Peter James. *The Economics of Anabaptism 1525-1560*. London: Mouton and Co., 1964.

Klippenstein, Lawrence, and Julius G. Toews, eds. *Manitoba Mennonite Memories*. Altona: Manitoba Mennonite Centennial Committee, 1974.

_____. *Mennonite Memories: Settling in Western Canada*. Winnipeg: Centennial Publications, 1977.

Loewen, Royden K. *Family, Church, and Market: A Mennonite Community in the Old and New Worlds, 1850-1930.* Toronto: University of Toronto Press, 1993.

Pannabecker, Samuel F. *Open Doors: A History of the General Conference Mennonite Church.* Newton: Faith and Life Press, 1975.

Smith, C. Henry. *The Story of the Mennonites.* Newton: Mennonite Publication Office, 1950.

Sprunger, Keith L. "God's Powerful Army of the Weak: Anabaptist Women of the Radical Reformation." In *Triumph Over Silence, Women in Protestant History.* Edited by Richard L. Greaves. Westport: Greenwood Press, 1985.

Toews, John A. *A History of the Mennonite Brethren Church.* Fresno: General Conference of Mennonite Brethren Churches, 1975.

Toews, John B. *Czars, Soviets and Mennonites.* Newton: Faith and Life Press, 1982.

Urry, James. *None But Saints: The Transformation of Mennonite Life in Russia 1789-1889.* Winnipeg: Hyperion Press, 1989.

Verheyden, A.L.E. *Anabaptism in Flanders, 1530-1650: A Century of Struggle.* Scottdale: Herald Press, 1961.

Wiebe, Walter, ed. *A Century of Grace and Witness (1860-1960).* Hillsboro: Mennonite Brethren Publishing House, 1960.

History of Mennonite Women

Baerg, Anna. *Diary of Anna Baerg (1916-1924).* Translated and edited by Gerald Peters. Winnipeg: Canadian Mennonite Brethren Bible College, 1985.

Bartel, Mary. *Saskatchewan Women in Mission* N.p.: Saskatchewan Women in Mission, 1977.

Born, Hilda J. "Plant Trees Wherever You Go: Katharina Zacharias Martens (1867-1929)," pp. 129-42. In *Women Among the Brethren.* Edited by Katie Funk Wiebe. Hillsboro: Mennonite Brethren Publishing House, 1979.

Cummings, Mary Lou, ed. *Full Circle: Stories of Mennonite Women.* Newton: Faith and Life Press, 1978.

Dyck, Anna Reimer. *Anna: From the Caucasus to Canada.* Translated and edited by Peter J. Klassen. Hillsboro: Mennonite Brethren Publishing House, 1979.

Epp, Marlene. "Women in Canadian Mennonite History: Uncovering the 'Underside.' " *Journal of Mennonite Studies* 5 (1987): 90-107.

Fiss, Hildegard. *The Story of Women in Mission (Southwest Ontario).* N.p., 1976.

Froese, Anita. *Manitoba Mennonite Women in Mission (1942-1977).* Winnipeg: Manitoba Mennonite Women in Mission, 1977.

Goering, Gladys V. *Women in Search of Mission: A History of the General Conference Mennonite Women's Organization.* Newton: Faith and Life Press, 1980.

Hooge, Katie. *The History of the Canadian Women in Mission (1952-1977).* Winnipeg: Canadian Women in Mission, 1977.

Klassen, Pamela E. *Going by the Moon and the Stars: Stories of Two Russian Mennonite Women.* Waterloo: Wilfrid Laurier University Press, 1994.

Neufeld, Anne, ed. *History of Alberta Mennonite Women in Mission (1947-1977).* Coaldale: Alberta Mennonite Women in Mission, 1977.

Neufeld, Nettie and Jessie Peters. *Fifty Years Ebenezer Verein 1936-1986.* Steinbach: Ebenezer *Verein,* 1987.

Ontario Women in Mission (1946-1986). N.p.: Ontario Women in Mission, 1986.

Rempel, Martha. *History of B.C. Mennonite Women in Mission (1939-1976).* Chilliwack: British Columbia Mennonite Women in Mission, 1976.

Thiessen, Anna. *The City Mission in Winnipeg.* Translated by Ida Toews. Winnipeg: Centre for MB Studies, 1991.

Toews, Margaret Gossen, ed. *South Western Ontario Women in Mission (1925-1987).* Leamington: South Western Ontario Women in Mission, 1987.

Toews, Susan. *Letters From Susan: A Woman's View of the Russian Mennonite Experience (1928-1941).* Translated and edited by John B. Toews. North Newton: Bethel College, 1988.

Unrau, Ruth. *Encircled: Stories of Mennonite Women.* Newton: Faith and Life Press, 1986.

Wiebe, Katie Funk. *Women Among the Brethren.* Hillsboro: Mennonite Brethren Publishing House, 1979.

_____. "Women in the Mennonite Brethren Church." In *Your Daughters Shall Prophesy: Women in Ministry in the Church.* Edited by John E. Toews et al. Winnipeg: Kindred Press, 1992.

History of Other Canadian Church Women

Bradbrook, Pauline. "A Brief Account of The Church of England Women's Association in Newfoundland." *Journal of the Canadian Church Historical Society* 28, 2 (October 1986): 92-105.

Brouwer, Ruth Compton ."The 'Between-Age' Christianity of Agnes Machar," *Canadian Historical Review* 65, 3 (1984): 347-370.

_____. *New Women for God: Canadian Presbyterian Women and India Missions, 1876-1914.* Toronto: University of Toronto Press, 1990.

_____. "Transcending the 'unacknowledged quarantine': Putting Religion into English-Canadian Women's History." *Journal of Canadian Studies* 27, 3 (Fall 1992): 47-61.

Campbell, Jean G. *A Lively Story: Historical Sketches of the Women's*

Missionary Society (Western Division) of the Presbyterian Church in Canada 1864-1989. N.p., 1989.

Caron, Anita, ed. *Femmes et pouvoir dans l'Église.* Montréal: VLB Éditeur, 1991.

Cramp, Mary. *Retrospect, A History of the Formation and Progress of the Women's Missionary Aid Societies of the Maritime Provinces.* N.p., 1892.

D'Allaire, Micheline. *Les Dots des religieuses au Canada français, 1639-1800. Étude économique et sociale.* Montréal: Hurtubise HMH, 1986.

Danylewyca, Marta. *Taking the Veil: An Alternative to Marriage, Motherhood, and Spinsterhood in Quebec, 1840-1920.* Toronto: McClelland and Stewart, 1987.

Davy, Shirley, Project Coordinator. *Women, Work and Worship in the United Church of Canada.* N.p.: The United Church of Canada, 1983.

Forbes, Jean Gordon. *Wide Windows: The Story of the Woman's Missionary Society of the United Church of Canada.* N.p.: Woman's Missionary Society, 1951.

Gagan, Rosemary. *A Sensitive Independence: Canadian Methodist Women Missionaries in Canada and the Orient, 1881-1925.* Kingston and Montreal: McGill-Queen's University Press, 1992.

Graham, Mrs. W. H. *Forty-Five Years Effort of the Woman's Missionary Society of the Methodist Church of Canada, 1881-1925.* Toronto: Woman's Missionary Society, n.d.

Hall, Nancy. "The Professionalisation of Women Workers in the Methodist, Presbyterian, and United Churches of Canada." In *First Days Fighting Days: Women in Manitoba History,* pp. 120-33. Edited by Mary Kinnear. Regina: Canadian Plains Research Center, 1987.

Hallett, Mary E. "Nellie McClung and the Fight for the Ordination of Women in the United Church of Canada." *Atlantis* 4, 2 (Spring 1979): 2-16.

Hancock, Carol L. "Nellie L. McClung: A Part of a Pattern." In *Prairie Spirit: Perspectives on the Heritage of the United Church of Canada in the West.* Edited by Dennis L. Butcher et al. Winnipeg: University of Manitoba Press, 1985.

Ingraham, Mary Kinley. *Seventy-Five Years Historical Sketch of the United Baptist Woman's Missionary Union in the Maritime Provinces of Canada.* Kentville: Kentville Publishing, n.d.

Johnson, Geoffrey. "The Road to Winsome Womanhood: The Canadian Presbyterian Mission among East Indian Women and Girls in Trinidad, 1868-1939." In *Canadian Protestant and Catholic Missions, 1820s-1960s: Historical Essays in Honour of John Webster Grant.* Edited by John S. Moir and C.T. McIntire. New York: Peter Lang, 1988.

Kemper, Alison. "Deaconess as Urban Missionary and Ideal Woman: Church of England Initiatives in Toronto, 1890-1895," In *Canadian Protestant and*

Catholic Missions, 1820s-1960s: Historical Essays in Honour of John Webster Grant. Edited by John S. Moir and C.T. McIntire. New York: Peter Lang, 1988.

Korinek, Valerie J. "No Women Need Apply: The Ordination of Women in the United Church, 1918-65." *Canadian Historical Review* 74, 4 (1993): 473-509.

Lacelle, Elisabeth J., éd. *La femme et la religion au Canada français.* Montréal: Bellarmin, 1979.

Laurin, Nicole; Danielle Juteau, and Lorraine Duchesne. *À la recherche d'un monde oublié. Les communautés religieuses de femmes au Québec de 1900 à 1970.* Montréal: Le Jour, 1991.

Les Ursulines de Québec, 1639-1989. Québec: Le Comité de Fêtes du 350e anniversaire du fondation de l'École des Ursulines de Québec, 1989.

McGuire, Sister Rita. *Marguerite d'Youville: A Pioneer for Our Times.* Ottawa: Novalis, 1982.

McKerihen, Mary. *A Brief History Relative to the Growth and Development of Woman's Associations from Local to Presbytery to Conference to Dominion Courts. 1913-1943.* Toronto: Woman's Association Council of the United Church of Canada, 1943.

McPherson, Margaret E. "Head, heart and purse: The Presbyterian Women's Missionary Society in Canada, 1876-1925." In *Prairie Spirit: Perspectives on the Heritage of the United Church of Canada in the West,* pp. 147-170. Edited by Dennis L. Butcher et al. Winnipeg: University of Manitoba Press, 1985.

Merrick, Earl. *These Impossible Women. The Story of the United Baptist Women's Missionary Union of the Atlantic Provinces.* Fredericton: N.p., 1970

Mitchinson, Wendy. "Canadian Women and the Church Missionary Societies in the Nineteenth Century: A Step Towards Independence." *Atlantis* 2 (Spring 1977): 58-75.

Morgan, Cecilia. "Gender, Religion, and Rural Society: Quaker Women in Norwich, Ontario, 1820-1880." *Ontario History* 82, 4 (December 1990): 273-287.

Muir, Elizabeth. "The Bark Schoolhouse: Methodist Episcopal Missionary Women in Upper Canada, 1827-1833." In *Canadian Protestant and Catholic Missions, 1820s-1960s: Historical Essays in Honour of John Webster Grant.* Edited by John S. Moir and C.T. McIntire. New York: Peter Lang, 1988.

_____. *Petticoats in the Pulpit: Early Nineteenth-Century Methodist Women Preachers in Upper Canada.* Toronto: United Church Publishing House, 1991.

National Council of Women of Canada. *Women of Canada, Their Life and Work.* N.p.: National Council of Women of Canada, 1900; reprint ed.,

1956.

Paquette Gilberte. *Dans le sillage d'Élisabeth Bruyère*. Vanier: Les Éditions L'Interligne, 1993.

Platt, Mrs. Garfield Arthur. *The Story of the Woman's Auxiliary in the Diocese of Ontario: 1885-1961*. N.p., 1961.

Platt, Harriet Louise. *The Story of the Years: A History of the Woman's Missionary Society of the Methodist Church, Canada, 1881-1906*, 2 vols. Toronto: Woman's Missionary Society, 1908.

Robillard Denise. *Émilie Tavernier-Gamelin*. Montréal: Éditions du Méridien, 1988.

Rousseau, Francois. *La Croix et le scalpel. Histoire des Augustines et de l'Hôtel-Dieu de Québec I: 1639-1892*. Québec: Septentrion, 1989.

Sniatynski, Gillian. "UCW at 25: Marys or Marthas?" *The Observer* (1987): 30.

Whiteley, Marilyn. "Modest, Unaffected and Fully Consecrated: Lady Evangelists in Canadian Methodism, 1884-1900," Canadian Methodist Historical Society, *Papers* 6 (1987).

Whiteley, Marilyn Färdig. " 'Doing Just About What They Please': Ladies' Aids in Ontario Methodism." *Ontario History* 82 ,4 (December 1990): 300.

Wilson, Lois. *Turning the World Upside Down: A Memoir*. Toronto: Doubleday Canada, 1989.

Other Secondary Sources

Butler, Judith. *Gender Trouble: Feminism and the Subversion of Identity*. New York: Routledge, 1990.

Davis, Natalie Zemon. " 'Women's History' in Transition: The European Case." *Feminist Studies* 3 (Spring-Summer 1976): 83-103.

French, Marilyn. *Beyond Power: On Women, Men and Morals*. New York: Ballantine Books, 1985.

Gordon, Ann D., Mari Jo Buhle, and Nancy Schrom Dye. "The Problem of Women's History." In *Liberating Women's History: Theoretical and Critical Essays*, pp. 75-91. Edited by Berenice A. Carroll. Chicago: University of Illinois Press, 1976.

Grant, John Webster. *The Church in the Canadian Era*. Burlington: Welch Publishing Company Inc., 1988.

Iggers, Georg G., and Harold T. Parker, eds. *International Handbook of Historical Studies: Contemporary Research and Theory*. Westport: Greenwood Press, 1975.

Jaggar, Alison M., and Paula Rothenberg Struhl. *Feminist Frameworks: Alternative Theoretical Accounts of the Relations between Women and Men*. New York: McGraw-Hill, 1978.

Kader, Soha Abdel. "The Role of Women in the History of the Arab States." In *Retrieving Women's History: Changing Perceptions of the Role of*

Women in Politics and Society. Edited by Jay S. Kleinberg. Great Britain: Berg Publishers Limited, 1988.

Kelly, Joan. *Women, History & Theory: The Essays of Joan Kelly.* Chicago: University of Chicago Press, 1984.

Lerner, Gerda. "New Approaches to the Study of Women in American History." In *Liberating Women's History: Theoretical and Critical Essays*, pp. 349-55. Edited by Berenice A. Carroll. Chicago: University of Illinois Press, 1976.

_____. "Placing Women in History: A 1975 Perspective." In *Liberating Women's History: Theoretical and Critical Essays*, pp. 357-67. Edited by Berenice A. Carroll. Chicago: University of Illinois Press, 1976.

Pierson, Ruth, and Alison Prentice. "Feminism and the Writing and Teaching of History." *Atlantis* 7, 2 (Spring/Printemps 1982): 37-46.

Pleck, Elizabeth H. "Women's History: Gender as a Category of Historical Analysis." In *Ordinary People and Everyday Life: Perspectives on the New Social History*, pp. 51-63. Edited by James B. Gardner and George Rollie Adams. Nashville: American Association for State and Local History, 1983.

Prentice, Alison, Paula Bourne, Gail Cuthbert Brandt, Beth Light, Wendy Mitchinson, and Naomi Black. *Canadian Women: A History.* Toronto: Harcourt Brace Jovanovich Canada, 1988.

Riley, Denise. *"Am I that Name?" Feminism and the Category of "Women" in History.* Minneapolis: University of Minnesota, 1988.

Scott, Joan Wallach. *Gender and the Politics of History.* New York: Columbia University Press, 1988.

_____. "The Problem of Invisibility." In *Retrieving Women's History: Changing Perceptions of the Role of Women in Politics and Society.* Edited by Jay S. Kleinberg. Great Britain: Berg Publishers, 1988.

Silverman, Elaine Leslau. "Writing Canadian Women's History, 1970-82: An Historiographical Analysis." *Canadian Historical Review* 63, 4 (1982): 513-33.

Smith, Hilda. "Feminism and the Methodology of Women's History." In *Liberating Women's History: Theoretical and Critical Essays*, pp. 368-84. Edited by Berenice A. Carroll. Chicago: University of Illinois Press, 1976.

Smith-Rosenberg, Carroll. "The New Woman and the New History." *Feminist Studies* 3 (1975): 185-98.

Stearns, Peter, N. "The New Social History: An Overview." In *Ordinary People and Everyday Life: Perspectives on the New Social History*, pp. 3-21. Edited by James B. Gardner and George Rollie Adams. Nashville: American Association for State and Local History, 1983.

Index

Abendkränzchen, 48

Acculturation of Mennonite women to society, 32, 123-24

Alberta Women in Mission, 130

Altona Mennonite Ladies Auxiliary, 103

Anabaptist Movement, 1

Anabaptist women's role, 25-31

Arelee MB Women's Missionary Fellowship, 90

Arnaud Christian Fellowship, 69, 90, 92

Auxiliary status, 35, 107

Baptist Church, women's role, 12, 41; Hannah Maria Norris, 41

Bargen, Anne, 60

Bergthal Mennonite Church, 65, 70

Bethel Church, 99

Bethel Ladies Aid, 99

Bethel Mennonite Church Women in Mission, 129

Biblical interpretation, 78, 104

Biblical motivation for Mennonite women's societies, 41, 43, 97, 111, 125

Biblical texts as mottos, 43, 71-73, 92-93, 112-13, 126 n.3

Blumenkränzchen, 49

Board of Foreign Missions of North America, 45

Boissevain Women in Mission, 92

Bradbrook, Pauline, 12

Brouwer, Ruth Compton, 9, 12, 18-19

Bruderschaft, 29, 39, 83

Busy Bees Circle, 48, 66

Busy Fingers Sewing Circle, 65, 67

Canadian Conference of MB Churches, 1, 4

Canadian Women in Mission (CWM), 3, 69-70, 93, 99-100, 105, 107, 125; the name, 6 n.12, 94 n.2, 103; twentieth anniversary, 11

Catherine the Great, 28

Central MB Church, 3, 98

Change in Mennonite women's societies, 78-79, 98, 132; in naming, 66, 89-92, 114-15; increase in numbers, 65-66; in needs, 105; because of education and career, 77-78, 105-106; because of employment outside the home, 77-78, 105-106, 121-22, 124; because of increased church involvement, 121-23, 126, 129-30; because of involvements outside the church, 122-24; from use of German to English, 123-24.

Christian Fellowship, 67-68

Christian Fellowship Guild, 68

Christian Service Club, 49, 68

Church dinners, catering, 105-20, 132

Church of England, Anglican Church: support of missions, 10-12, 40; Women's Auxiliary to the Board of Missions of the Church of England in Canada, 11

Church Women, 91

Church women's societies other than Mennonite, 10, 65; male control of, 10, 12, 18, 39; naming of, 46-47; auction sales in, 46; support of missions in, 40.

Coaldale Mennonite Church, 69

Concordia Ladies Aid, 15

Conference of MB Churches of Ontario, 62

Conference of Mennonites in Canada (CMC), 1-4; establishment of, 31-32

Conference themes of Mennonite women's societies, 73, 92

Conrad Grebel College, 130

Constitutions of Mennonite women's societies, 3, 69, 91, 117

Contribution of Mennonite women's societies, 10-14, 62, 99

Criticism of Mennonite women's societies, 42-43

Series Published by Wilfrid Laurier University Press for the Canadian Corporation for Studies in Religion / Corporation Canadienne des Sciences Religieuses

Editions SR

1. *La langue de Ya'udi : description et classement de l'ancien parler de Zencircli dans le cadre des langues sémitiques du nord-ouest*
   Paul-Eugène Dion, O.P.
   1974 / viii + 511 p. / OUT OF PRINT
2. *The Conception of Punishment in Early Indian Literature*
   Terence P. Day
   1982 / iv + 328 pp. / OUT OF PRINT
3. *Traditions in Contact and Change: Selected Proceedings of the XIVth Congress of the International Association for the History of Religions*
   Edited by Peter Slater and Donald Wiebe with Maurice Boutin and Harold Coward
   1983 / x + 758 pp. / OUT OF PRINT
4. *Le messianisme de Louis Riel*
   Gilles Martel
   1984 / xviii + 483 p.
5. *Mythologies and Philosophies of Salvation in the Theistic Traditions of India*
   Klaus K. Klostermaier
   1984 / xvi + 549 pp. / OUT OF PRINT
6. *Averroes' Doctrine of Immortality: A Matter of Controversy*
   Ovey N. Mohammed
   1984 / vi + 202 pp. / OUT OF PRINT
7. *L'étude des religions dans les écoles : l'expérience américaine, anglaise et canadienne*
   Fernand Ouellet
   1985 / xvi + 666 p.
8. *Of God and Maxim Guns: Presbyterianism in Nigeria, 1846-1966*
   Geoffrey Johnston
   1988 / iv + 322 pp.
9. *A Victorian Missionary and Canadian Indian Policy: Cultural Synthesis vs Cultural Replacement*
   David A. Nock
   1988 / x + 194 pp. / OUT OF PRINT
10. *Prometheus Rebound: The Irony of Atheism*
    Joseph C. McLelland
    1988 / xvi + 366 pp.
11. *Competition in Religious Life*
    Jay Newman
    1989 / viii + 237 pp.
12. *The Huguenots and French Opinion, 1685-1787: The Enlightenment Debate on Toleration*
    Geoffrey Adams
    1991 / xiv + 335 pp.
13. *Religion in History: The Word, the Idea, the Reality / La religion dans l'histoire : le mot, l'idée, la réalité*
    Edited by/Sous la direction de Michel Despland and/et Gérard Vallée
    1992 / x + 252 pp.
14. *Sharing Without Reckoning: Imperfect Right and the Norms of Reciprocity*
    Millard Schumaker
    1992 / xiv + 112 pp.

15. *Love and the Soul: Psychological Interpretations of the Eros and Psyche Myth*
    James Gollnick
    1992 / viii + 174 pp.
16. *The Promise of Critical Theology: Essays in Honour of Charles Davis*
    Edited by Marc P. Lalonde
    1995 / xii + 146 pp.
17. *The Five Aggregates: Understanding Theravāda Psychology and Soteriology*
    Mathieu Boisvert
    1995 / xii + 166 pp.
18. *Mysticism and Vocation*
    James R. Horne
    1996 / vi + 110 pp.
19. *Memory and Hope: Strands of Canadian Baptist History*
    Edited by David T. Priestley
    1996 / viii + 211 pp.

Comparative Ethics Series /
Collection d'Éthique Comparée

1. *Muslim Ethics and Modernity: A Comparative Study of the Ethical Thought
   of Sayyid Ahmad Khan and Mawlana Mawdudi*
   Sheila McDonough
   1984 / x + 130 pp. / OUT OF PRINT
2. *Methodist Education in Peru: Social Gospel, Politics, and American
   Ideological and Economic Penetration, 1888-1930*
   Rosa del Carmen Bruno-Jofré
   1988 / xiv + 223 pp.
3. *Prophets, Pastors and Public Choices: Canadian Churches and the
   Mackenzie Valley Pipeline Debate*
   Roger Hutchinson
   1992 / xiv + 142 pp. / OUT OF PRINT

Dissertations SR

1. *The Social Setting of the Ministry as Reflected in the Writings
   of Hermas, Clement and Ignatius*
   Harry O. Maier
   1991 / viii + 230 pp. / OUT OF PRINT
2. *Literature as Pulpit: The Christian Social Activism of Nellie L. McClung*
   Randi R. Warne
   1993 / viii + 236 pp.

Studies in Christianity and Judaism /
Études sur le christianisme et le judaïsme

1. *A Study in Anti-Gnostic Polemics: Irenaeus, Hippolytus, and Epiphanius*
   Gérard Vallée
   1981 / xii + 114 pp. / OUT OF PRINT
2. *Anti-Judaism in Early Christianity*
   Vol. 1, *Paul and the Gospels*, edited by Peter Richardson with David Granskou
   1986 / x + 232 pp.
   Vol. 2, *Separation and Polemic*
   Edited by Stephen G. Wilson
   1986 / xii + 185 pp.
3. *Society, the Sacred, and Scripture in Ancient Judaism: A Sociology of Knowledge*
   Jack N. Lightstone
   1988 / xiv + 126 pp.

4. *Law in Religious Communities in the Roman Period: The Debate Over* **Torah** *and* **Nomos** *in Post-Biblical Judaism and Early Christianity*
   Peter Richardson and Stephen Westerholm with A. I. Baumgarten,
   Michael Pettem and Cecilia Wassén
   1991 / x + 164 pp.
5. *Dangerous Food: 1 Corinthians 8-10 in Its Context*
   Peter D. Gooch
   1993 / xviii + 178 pp.
6. *The Rhetoric of the Babylonian Talmud, Its Social Meaning and Context*
   Jack N. Lightstone
   1994 / xiv + 317 pp.

The Study of Religion in Canada /
Sciences Religieuses au Canada

1. *Religious Studies in Alberta: A State-of-the-Art Review*
   Ronald W. Neufeldt
   1983 / xiv + 145 pp.
2. *Les sciences religieuses au Québec depuis 1972*
   Louis Rousseau et Michel Despland
   1988 / 158 p.
3. *Religious Studies in Ontario: A State-of-the-Art Review*
   Harold Remus, William Closson James and Daniel Fraikin
   1992 / xviii + 422 pp.
4. *Religious Studies in Manitoba and Saskatchewan: A State-of-the-Art Review*
   John M. Badertscher, Gordon Harland and Roland E. Miller
   1993 / vi + 166 pp.
5. *The Study of Religion in British Columbia: A State-of-the-Art Review*
   Brian J. Fraser
   1995 / x + 127 pp.

Studies in Women and Religion /
Études sur les femmes et la religion

1. *Femmes et religions**
   Sous la direction de Denise Veillette
   1995 / xviii + 466 p.
   * Only available from Les Presses de l'Université Laval
2. *The Work of Their Hands: Mennonite Women's Societies in Canada*
   Gloria Neufeld Redekop
   1996 / xvi + 172 pp.
3. *Profiles of Anabaptist Women: Sixteenth-Century Reforming Pioneers*
   Edited by C. Arnold Snyder and Linda A. Huebert Hecht
   1996 / xxii + 438 pp.

SR Supplements

1. *Footnotes to a Theology: The Karl Barth Colloquium of 1972*
   Edited and Introduced by Martin Rumscheidt
   1974 / viii + 151 pp. / OUT OF PRINT
2. *Martin Heidegger's Philosophy of Religion*
   John R. Williams
   1977 / x + 190 pp. / OUT OF PRINT
3. *Mystics and Scholars: The Calgary Conference on Mysticism 1976*
   Edited by Harold Coward and Terence Penelhum
   1977 / viii + 121 pp. / OUT OF PRINT

Available from:

WILFRID LAURIER UNIVERSITY PRESS
Waterloo, Ontario, Canada   N2L 3C5